Franz
<u>LISZT</u>

DIE IDEALE
Symphonic Poem No. 12
S. 106

Study Score
Partitur

PETRUCCI LIBRARY PRESS

INTRODUCTION

The present score is a reissue of one from the Franz Liszt-Stiftung edition, originally published by Breitkopf & Härtel from 1907-1936. The edition was prepared in an effort to publish the entire oeuvre of Franz Liszt. Editors included such prominent musicians as Béla Bartok, Ferruccio Busoni, Eugène d'Albert and José Vianna da Motta – some of whom studied with Liszt – as well as scholars like Peter Raabe, who would later compile the first catalog of the composer's works. The need for a complete edition was already apparent by the time of Liszt's death. Although some of his piano music had regularly appeared in new editions throughout his life, these works were by no means representative of even his pianistic output. A far more unfortunate fate was left for his orchestral music - which would usually be issued only once, soon to go out of print and later scarcely available. The Liszt-Stiftung edition revived many works that had fallen into relative obscurity and was therefore handsomely welcomed.

The edition was sadly never completed. The publication activity was brought to a premature end by the time of the Second World War. All in all the incomplete edition encompassed 34 volumes, among others two symphonies, the symphonic poems, some concert works, a couple of piano arrangements and 11 volumes of original works for piano – a mere fraction of the composer's output – but the edition would nonetheless break the ground for Liszt research during the 20th century for a number of reasons. First, it brought to light a number of late pieces that would put Liszt as a forerunner of experimental music and firmly establish his position as such. Second, it revealed the diversity of Liszt's output, which up until that time had been best known as an important addition to the piano repertoire. Third, it displayed the complex and characteristic nature of many of his works by being the first edition to show and make use of several alternative (sometimes vastly different) versions and sources. Last but not least, it would provide the world with a generally reliable edition of easy availability and very high standard for its day.

The Bavarian State Library acquired a complete copy of said edition and decided to digitize it in 2008. By that time more than 70 years had passed since its publication, effectively rendering the edition out of copyright and free for any use. Each and every page was scanned and uploaded to their online digital collection. While this was a great effort in itself, the site has a rudimentary interface, is difficult to navigate and the scores are not in the context of relevant information. One of our users decided to also upload it to our site, the International Music Score Library Project (IMSLP) / Petrucci Music Library, the unique wiki-based repository of musical scores, composers and indexes that anyone can edit and amend. Through the effort of a single user, Mattias K. (piupianissimo), the entire edition is now easily available worldwide to those who wish to perform and study the composer's music in a historical context, since as the case is with Liszt's music, many early editions exist and many are readily available on the site and many more will be available in the future. IMSLP is as such a valuable resource available to the scholar but even more to the performer who is always a mere mouse click away from scores that have not been in print since the turn of the past century, or that are otherwise hard to come by. The availability, quantity of ease of access for online scores will soon exceed those of the traditional medium of print. Nevertheless new works have always been published through the printed medium and this tradition is going to persist for many years to come even if complemented by the digital medium. Of course an important fact to stress is that the availability of digital scores online does not exclude the need of printed score since neither one can replace the comfort and neatness of one another. The quality of a bound reprint or new engraving exceeds that of a score printed at home.

I discovered IMSLP back in early 2006 when it first began. At that time many scores were scattered on the net either privately or on commercial collection sites. Many of these sites had a considerably large collection but sadly many had restrictions on number of downloads per day and the process of contributing to them was riddled with bureaucracy. IMSLP was the first free site where anyone could contribute and upload any kind of musical scores. I have personally searched and uploaded many works – particularly those of Liszt – and the future of the site is nothing but bright. At the time of its start only a handful of scores were available on the site but through the effort of its users IMSLP has grown to be the largest collection of scores available on the Internet.

Die Ideale is the twelfth work in a series of thirteen symphonic poems composed by Franz Liszt. It was composed from 1856-57 and first published in 1858 by Breitkopf und Härtel of Leipzig. The dedicatee is Princess Carolyne zu Sayn-Wittgenstein. This score is from the sixth volume of the Franz Liszt-Stiftung edition, edited by Otto Taubmann and published in 1910. The score, along with a number or arrangements, is also available directly at the following URL:
http:// imslp.org/wiki/Die_Ideale,_S.106_(Liszt,_Franz)

Soren Afshar (Funper)

Summer, 2011

COMPOSER'S PREFACE

Eine Aufführung, welche den Intentionen des Komponisten entsprechen und ihnen Klang, Farbe, Rhythmus und Leben verleihen soll, wird bei meinen Orchester-Werken am zweckmässigsten und mit dem geringsten Zeitverlust durch geteilte Vor-Proben gefördert werden. Demzufolge erlaube ich mir, die HH. Dirigenten, welche meine symphonischen Dichtungen aufzuführen beabsichtigen, zu ersuchen, der General-Probe Separat-Proben mit dem Streich-Quartett, andere mit Blas- und Schlag-Instrumenten vorangehen zu lassen.

Gleichzeitig sei mir gestattet zu bemerken, dass ich das mechanische, taktmässige, zerschnittene Auf- und Abspielen, wie es an manchen Orten noch üblich ist, möglichst beseitigt wünsche, und nur den periodischen Vortrag, mit dem Hervortreten der besonderen Accente und der Abrundung der melodischen und rhythmischen Nuanzierung, als sachgemäss anerkennen kann. In der geistigen Auffassung des Dirigenten liegt der Lebensnerv einer symphonischen Produktion, vorausgesetzt, dass im Orchester die geziemenden Mittel zu deren Verwirklichung sich vorfinden; andernfalls möchte es ratsamer erscheinen, sich nicht mit Werken zu befassen, welche keineswegs eine Alltags-Popularität beanspruchen.

Obschon ich bemüht war, durch genaue Anzeichnungen meine Intentionen zu verdeutlichen, so verhehle ich doch nicht, dass Manches, ja sogar das Wesentlichste, sich nicht zu Papier bringen lässt, und nur durch das künstlerische Vermögen, durch sympathisch schwungvolles Reproduzieren, sowohl des Dirigenten als der Aufführenden, zur durchgreifenden Wirkung gelangen kann. Dem Wohlwollen meiner Kunstgenossen sei es daher überlassen, das Meiste und Vorzüglichste an meinen Werken zu vollbringen.

Weimar, März 1856.

Pour obtenir un résultat d'exécution correspondant aux intentions de mes œuvres orchestrales, et leur donner le coloris, le rhythme, l'accent et la vie qu'elles réclament, il sera utile d'en préparer la répétition générale par des répétitions partielles des instruments à cordes, à vent, en cuivre, et à percussion. Par cette méthode de la division du travail on épargnera du temps en facilitant aux exécutants l'intelligence de l'ouvrage. Je me permets en conséquence de prier MM. les chefs d'orchestre qui seraient disposés à faire exécuter l'un de ces Poèmes symphoniques, de vouloir bien prendre le soin de faire précéder les répétitions générales, des répétitions préalables indiquées ci-dessus.

En même temps j'observerai que la mesure dans les œuvres de ce genre demande à être maniée avec plus de mesure, de souplesse, et d'intelligence des effets de coloris, de rhythme, et d'expression qu'il n'est encore d'usage dans beaucoup d'orchestres. Il ne suffit pas qu'une composition soit régulièrement bâtonnée et machinalement exécutée avec plus ou moins de correction pour que l'auteur ait à se louer de cette façon de propagation de son œuvre, et puisse y reconnaître une fidèle interprétation de sa pensée. Le nerf vital d'une belle exécution symphonique gît principalement dans la compréhension de l'œuvre reproduite, que le chef d'orchestre doit surtout posséder et communiquer, dans la manière de partager et d'accentuer les périodes, d'accuser les contrastes tout en ménageant les transitions de veiller tantôt à établir l'équilibre entre les divers instruments, tantôt à les faire ressortir soit isolément soit par groupes, car à tel moment il convient d'entonner ou de marquer simplement les notes, mais à d'autres il s'agit de phraser, de chanter, et même de déclamer. C'est au chef qu'il appartient d'indiquer à chacun des membres de l'orchestre la signification du rôle qu'il a à remplir.

Je me suis attaché à rendre mes intentions par rapport aux nuances, à l'accélération et au retard des mouvements, etc. aussi sensibles que possible par un emploi détaillé des signes et des expressions usitées; néanmoins ce serait une illusion de croire qu'on puisse fixer sur le papier ce qui fait la beauté et le caractère de l'exécution. Le talent et l'inspiration des artistes dirigeants et exécutants en ont seuls le secret, et la part de sympathie que ceux-ci voudront bien accorder à mes œuvres, seront pour elles le meilleur gage de succès.

Weimar, Mars 1856.

In order to secure a performance of my orchestral works which accords with their intentions, and which imparts to them the colour, rhythm, accent and life that they require, it is recommended that the general rehearsal should be preceded by separate rehearsals of the Strings, Wind, Brass, and instruments of percussion. By this division of labour time will be saved, and the executants will more rapidly be made familiar with what is required of them. I therefore venture to request that conductors, who are pleased to bring one or the other of my symphonic poems to a hearing will adopt the plan formulated above.

At the same time I may be allowed to remark that it is my wish that the mechanical, bar by bar, up and down beating of time, which obtains in so many places, should as far as possible be discarded, and that only the periodic divisions, with the prominence of certain accentuation and the rounding off of melodic and rhythmical nuances should alone be regarded as indispensable. The vitality of a symphonic performance depends upon the intellectual perception of the conductor, presuming that suitable material for its realisation is to be found in the orchestra; failing this it would seem to be advisable to hold aloof from works which do not claim a promise of every-day popularity.

Although I have endeavoured to make my intentions clear by providing exact marks of expression, I cannot conceal from myself that much, and that perhaps the most important, cannot be set forth on paper, but can only be successfully brought to light by the artistic capability and the sympathetic and enthusiastic reproduction by both conductor and executants. It may therefore be left to my colleagues in art to do the most and best that they can for my works.

Weimar. March 1856.

F. Liszt.

After the 1854 relief by Ernst Rietschel

INSTRUMENTATION

2 Flutes

2 Oboes

2 Clarinets

2 Bassoons

4 Horns

2 Trumpets

3 Trombones

Tuba

Timpani

Cymbals

Violins I

Violins II

Violas

Violoncellos

Basses

Duration: ca. 30 minutes

First Performance: September 5, 1854
Weimar: Hofkapelle
Franz Liszt, conductor

ISBN: 978-1-60874-032-1

This score is an unabridged reprint of the score
first issued in Leipzig by Breitkopf & Härtel, 1910. Plate F.L. 12

Printed in the USA
First Printing: December, 2011

DIE IDEALE
Symphonic Poem No. 12
S. 106

Die Ideale.
(Friedrich v. Schiller.)

So willst du treulos von mir scheiden
Mit deinen holden Phantasien,
Mit deinen Schmerzen, deinen Freuden,
Mit allen unerbittlich fliehn?
Kann nichts dich, Fliehende, verweilen,
O meines Lebens goldne Zeit?
Vergebens! deine Wellen eilen
Hinab ins Meer der Ewigkeit.
Erloschen sind die heitern Sonnen,
Die meiner Jugend Pfad erhellt;
Die Ideale sind zerronnen,
Die einst das trunkne Herz geschwellt.
. . . .

The Ideals.
(English translation by Harry Brett.)

Thus willst thou, faithless one, desert me,
With thine entrancing phantasy.
With joys untold and pains that hurt me,
With all these, unrelentless flee?
Can naught, o fickle one, compel thee
To stay? My guiding star to be?
'Tis hopeless! For thy waves impel thee
Forever towards Eternity.
The merry sun-rays all are banished
That made in youth my path so bright;
Now all ideals and hopes have vanished,
That once my swelling heart made light.
. . . .

Les Idéals.
(Version française par E. Montaubric.)

Ta joie et ta douleur et tes douces chimères
Tu veux me les ravir, infidèle, à jamais?
Sans pitié pour mon cœur et ses larmes amères,
Tu ne me laisses rien de tout ce que j'aimais!
Temps doré de ma vie, ô printemps, ô jeunesse,
Qu'est-ce qui pourrait bien te retenir captif?
Non, je l'invoque en vain! Riant de ma détresse,
Dans l'éternelle mer le cruel fugitif
Précipite sa course!... O rayon magnifique
Brillant à mon aurore: idéal, joie, amour,
Tu remplissais mon cœur d'une force magique,
Et maintenant, éteint et perdu sans retour.

FRANZ LISZT (1811–1886)

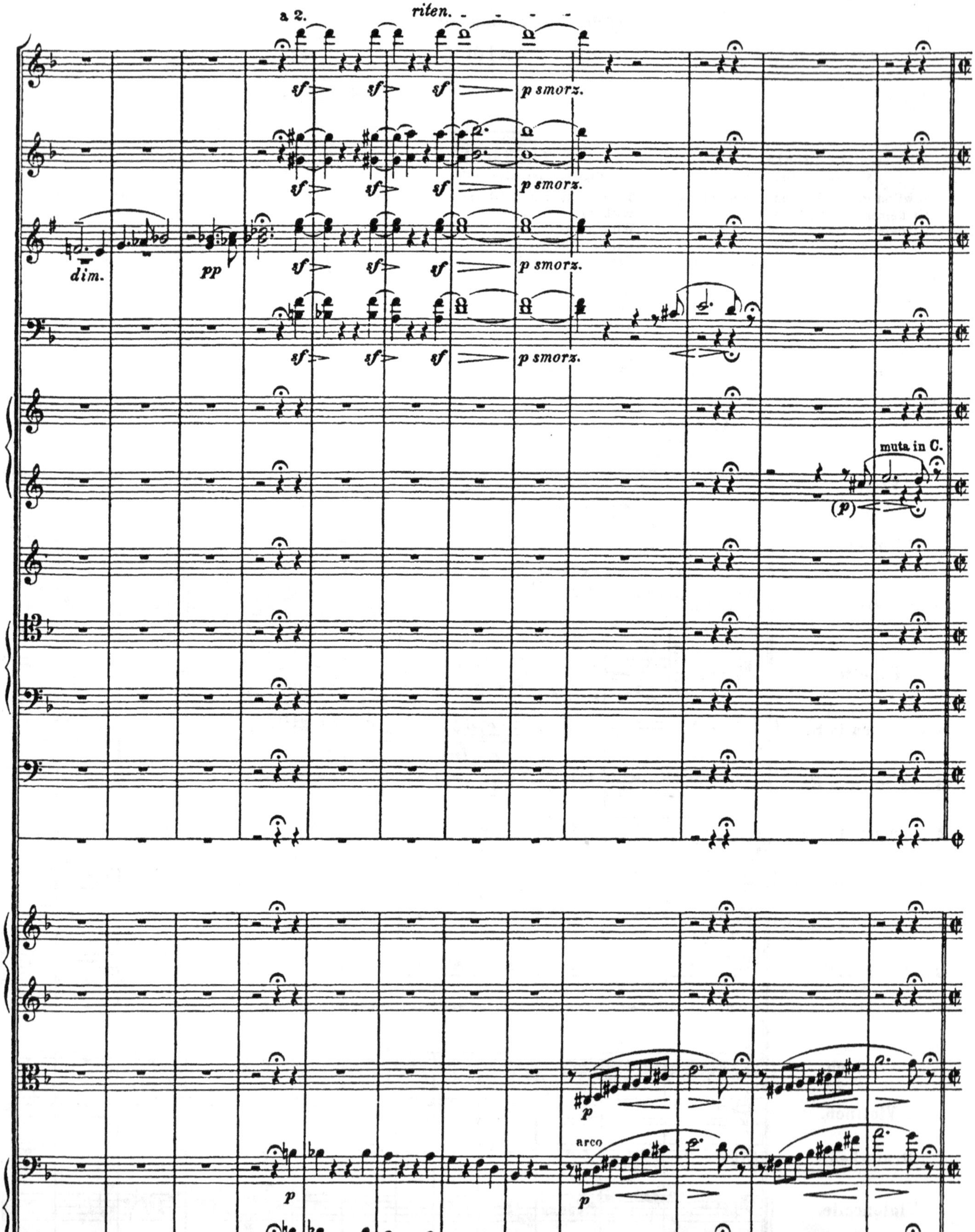
a 2.
riten.
sf
p smorz.
dim.
pp
muta in C.
(p)
p
arco
riten.

Aufschwung.

Es dehnte mit allmächt'gem Streben
Die enge Brust ein kreisend All,
Herauszutreten in das Leben,
In Tat und Wort, in Bild und Schall.

. . . .

Wie aus des Berges stillen Quellen
Ein Strom die Urne langsam füllt
Und jetzt mit königlichen Wellen
Die hohen Ufer überschwillt.
Es werfen Steine, Felsenlasten
Und Wälder sich in seine Bahn,
Er aber stürzt mit stolzen Masten
Sich rauschend in den Ocean:
So sprang, von kühnem Mut beflügelt,
Beglückt in seines Traumes Wahn,
Von keiner Sorge noch gezügelt.
Der Jüngling in des Lebens Bahn.
Bis an des Äthers bleichste Sterne
Erhob ihn der Entwürfe Flug;
Nichts war so hoch und nichts so ferne
Wohin ihr Flügel ihn nicht trug.

Aspirations.

Ah then how swelled with mighty longing
My bosom's bounds. It felt the need
To venture there where men were thronging,
And make my mark in word and deed.

. . . .

And as the mountain-spring's beginning
The urn but slowly fills at first,
Yet on its course, in volume winning,
O'er lofty banks at times will burst
While sturdy boulders, rocks high'-tow'ring
And woods in vain its course would stay,
It rushes on with force o'er-pow'ring
To ocean-depths it makes its way:
Thus rushed the youth in fond illusion,
With valor winged, his part to take
In life, as yet without intrusion
Of Care, his sanguine hopes to shake
Fair plans lent wings to pierce the azure,
And up to far-off stars to soar,
The distance thought he ne'er to measure
Illusions wing's him onwards bore.

Essor.

A mon esprit étroit la nature infinie
Donnait une puissante et forte impulsion,
L'entraînait vers la vie, aussi vers l'action
Et faisait naître en lui le rhythme et l'harmonie.

. . . .

Tel qu'on voit un torrent des flancs de la montagne
Sourde pour se frayer un pénible chemin,
Le voilà devenu, dans la verte campagne
Fleuve majestueux, supportant mal le frein
De ses bords élevés. Pierre, rocher informe,
Forêt avaient voulu modérer son élan:
Lui, triomphe toujours: dans l'océan énorme,
Tout fier des mâts, qu'il porte, il se jette, en grondant.
Tel, hardi, s'élançait sans craindre de barrière,
Le jeune homme fougueux, rempli d'illusion;
Il marchait, confiant, dans la vaste carrière,
De la beauté suprême ayant la vision.
Alors il se fiait à son aile légère,
Il quittait cette terre, il volait vers les cieux.
Des astres éloignés contemplait la lumière,
Qui des autres mortels ne frappe point les yeux.

A Allegro spiritoso. (Alla Breve.)

A Allegro spiritoso. (Alla Breve.)

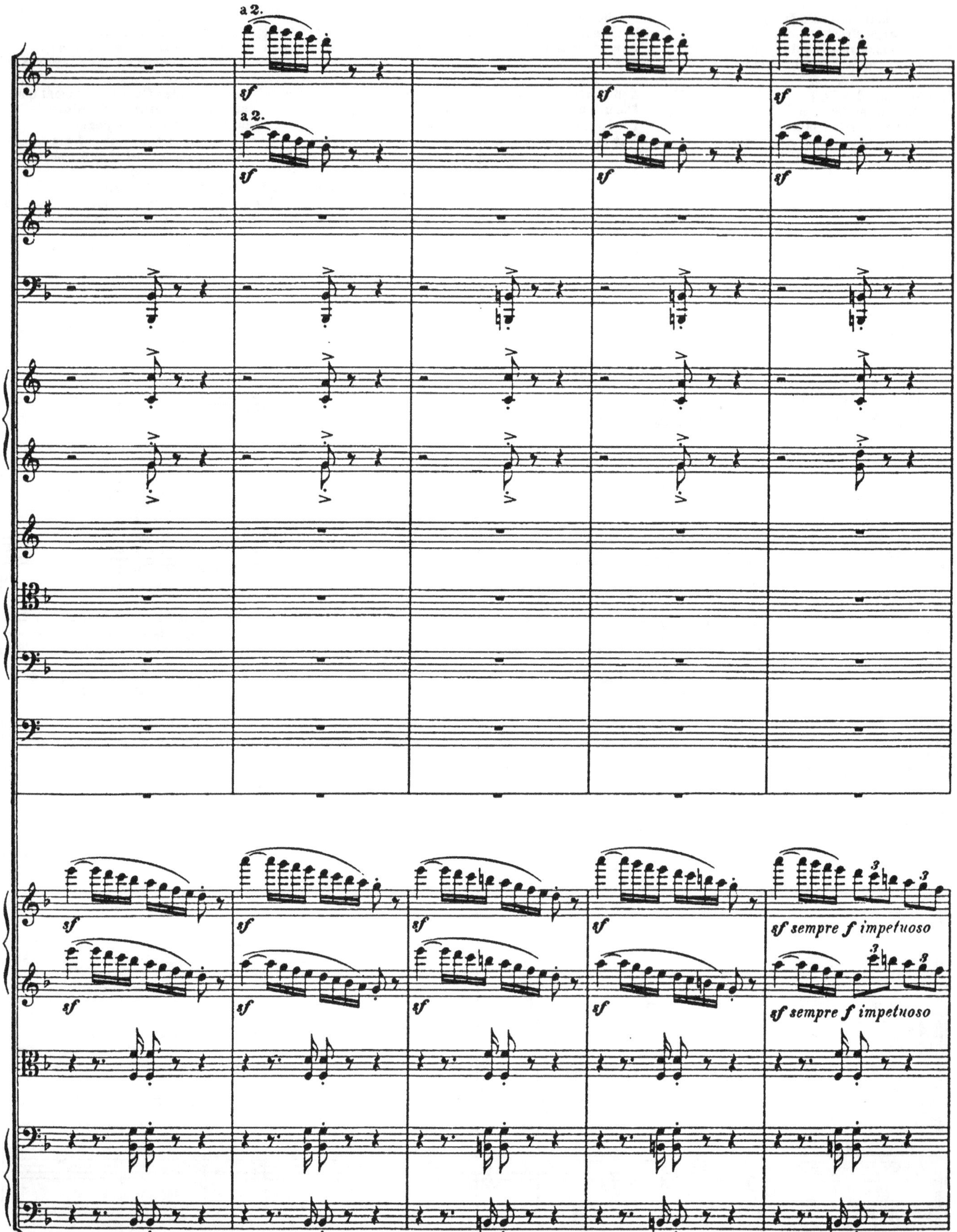
a 2.
sf
a 2.
sf
sf sempre f impetuoso
sf sempre f impetuoso

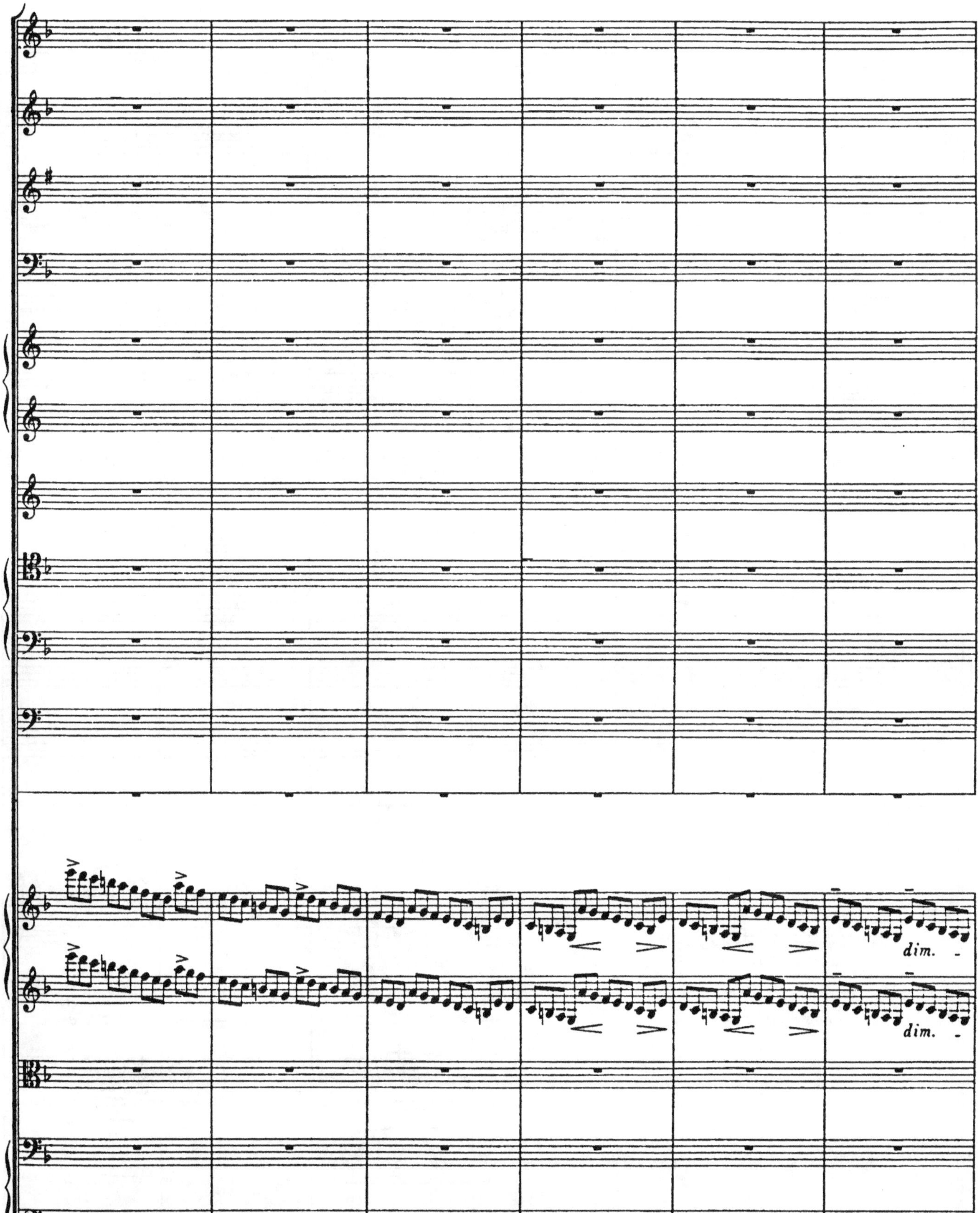
dim.
dim.

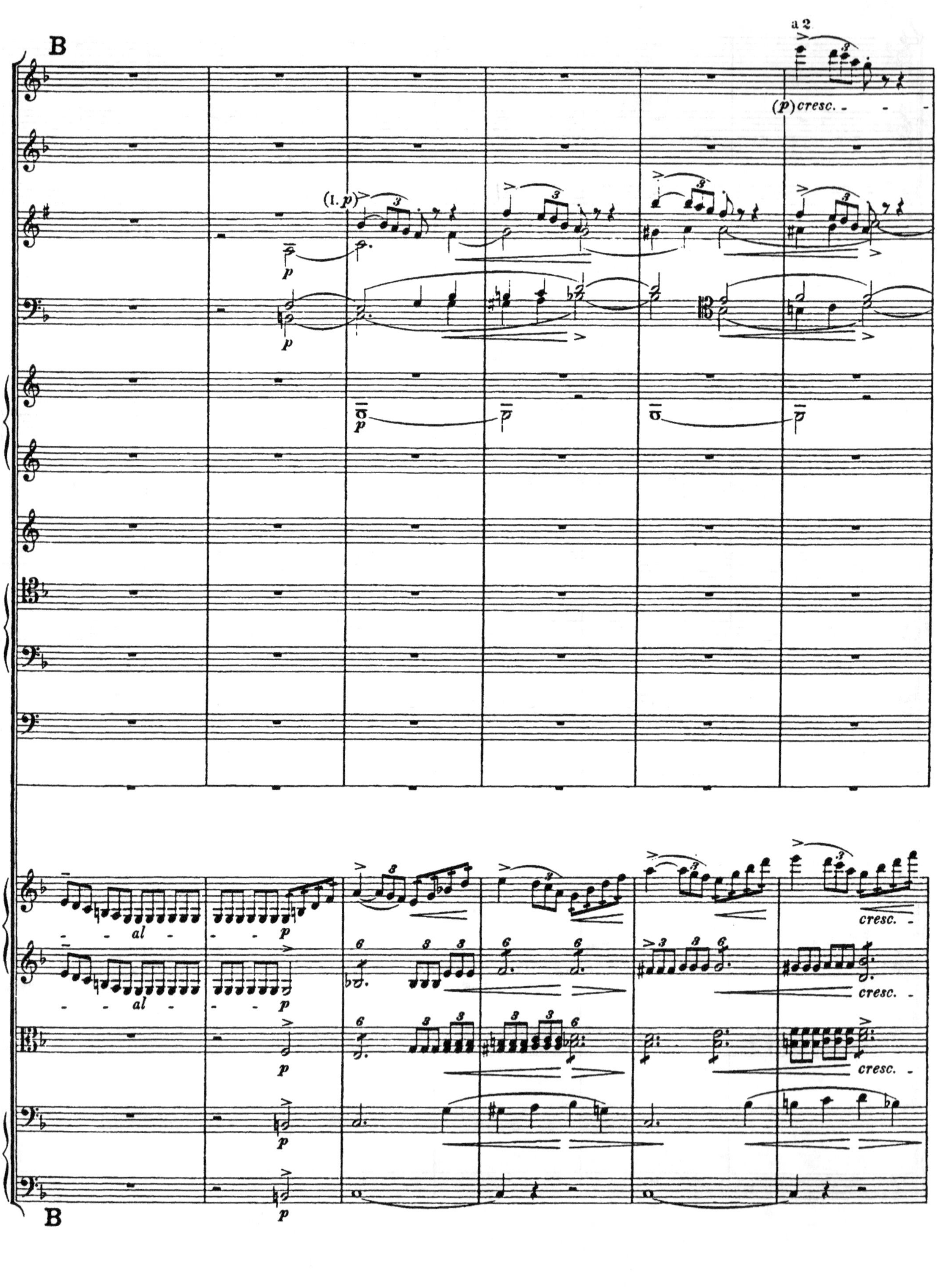
B
a 2
(p) cresc.
(I. p)
p
al
cresc.
B

a 2.
p subito
p
cresc.
p subito
cresc.
p subito
p
p subito
p subito
p subito
cresc.
rinforz.
p subito
p subito

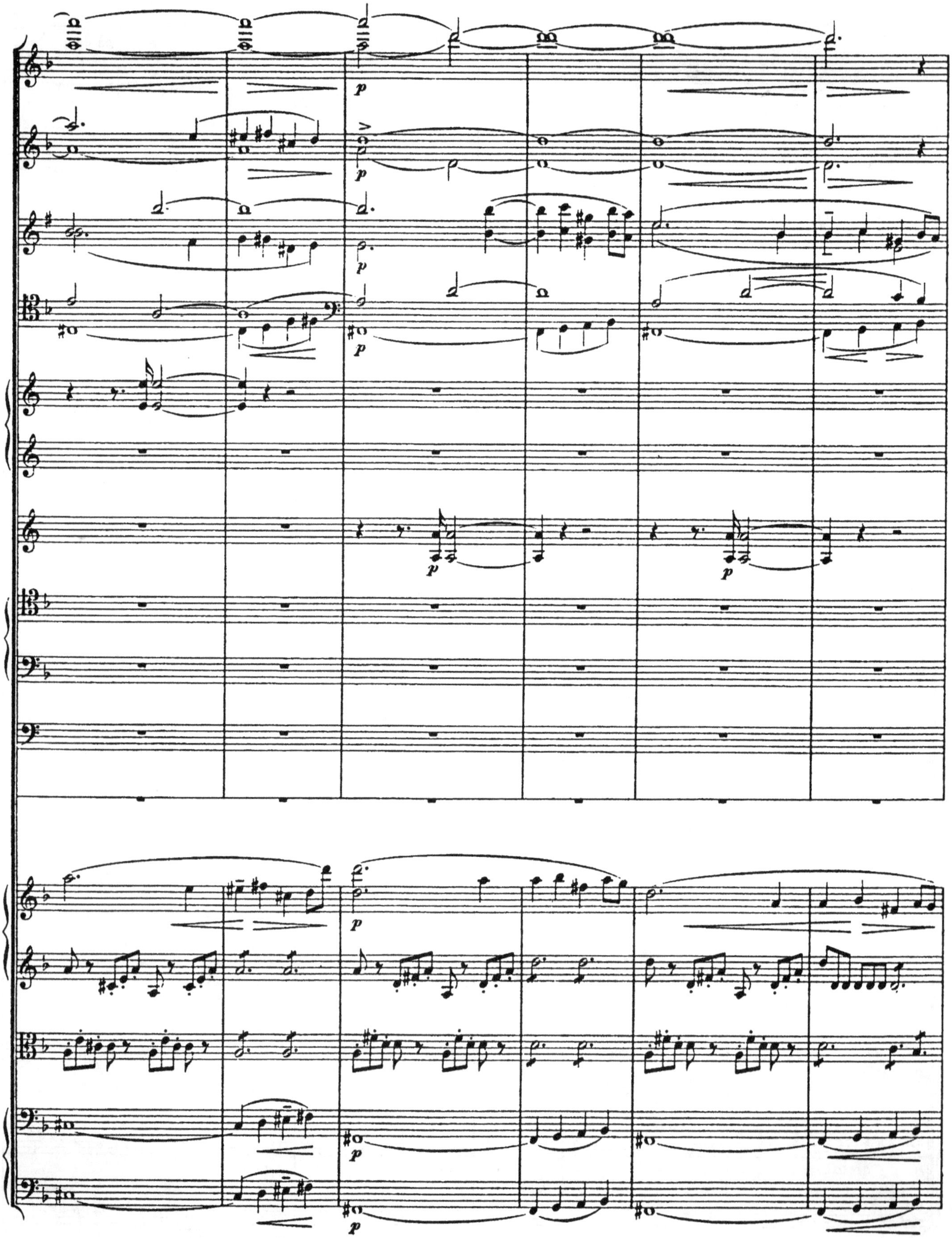

C
espressivo e cresc.
(cresc. - - - - - -)
espressivo e cresc.
cresc.
cresc.
cresc.
cresc.
C

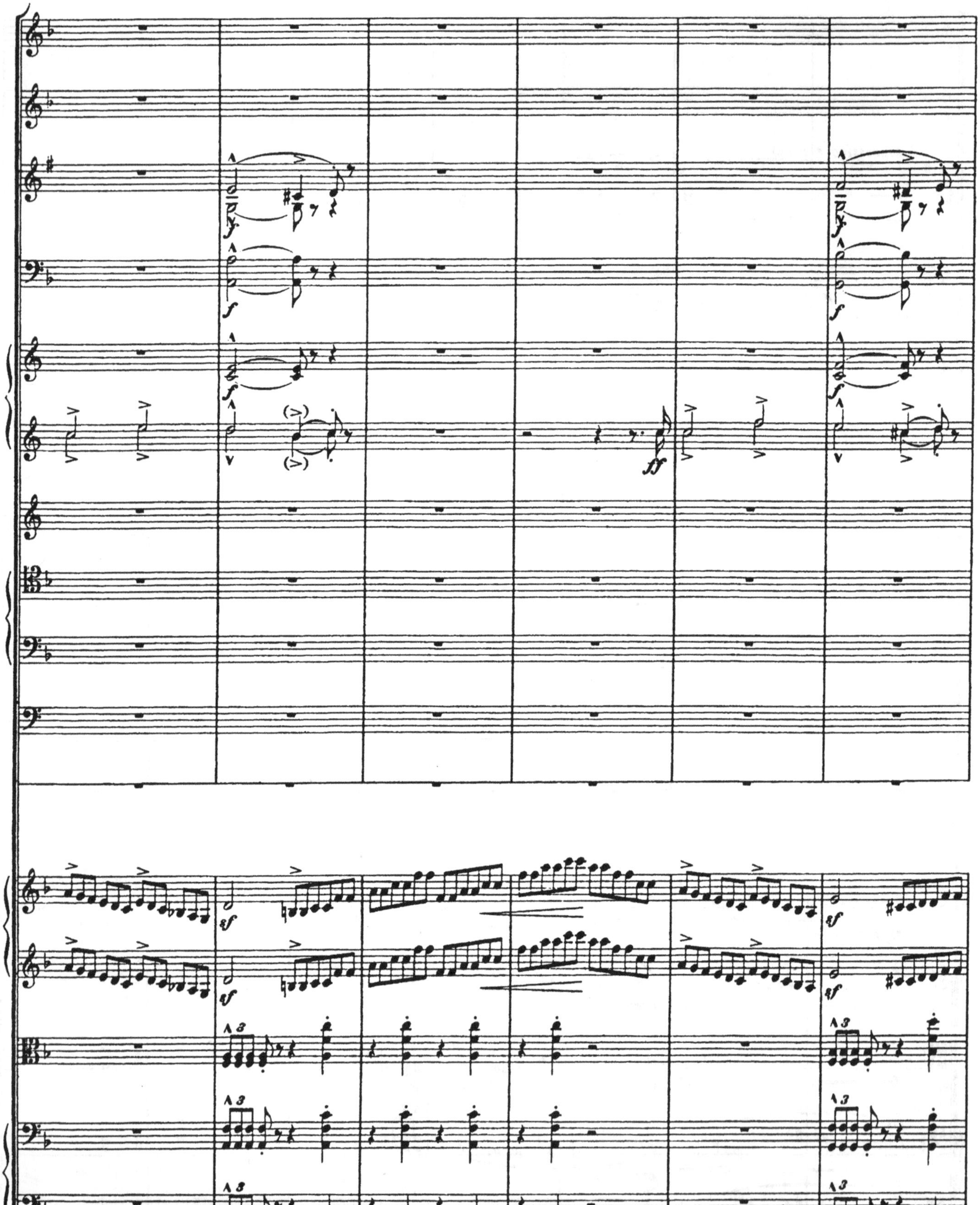
f
ff
sf

sempre f
sempre f
sempre f
sempre f
sempre f
sempre f
mf
div.
sempre ff
div.
cresc.
cresc.
sempre ff
sempre ff
cresc.
sempre ff
cresc.
sempre ff

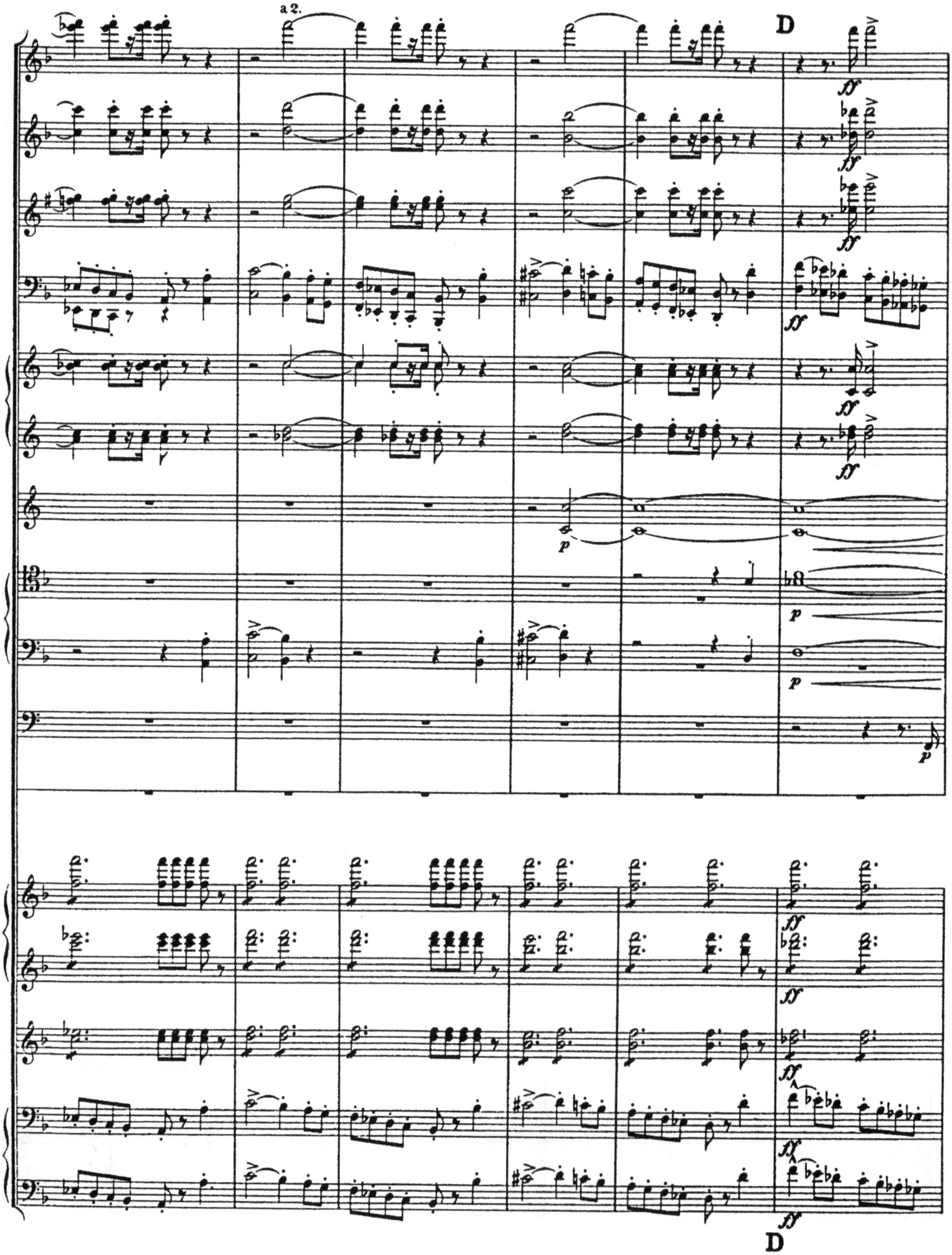
a 2.
D
ff
p
D

Die Buchstaben R.... und A.... bedeuten geringe Ritardando und Accelerando, so zu sagen: leise crescendo und diminuendo des Rhythmus.
The letters R.... and A.... signify slight Ritardando and Accelerando, so to speak: gentle crescendo and diminuendo of the rhythm.
Les lettres R.... et A.... signifient de petits Ritardando et Accelerando, c'est-à-dire: de doux crescendo et diminuendo du rhythme.

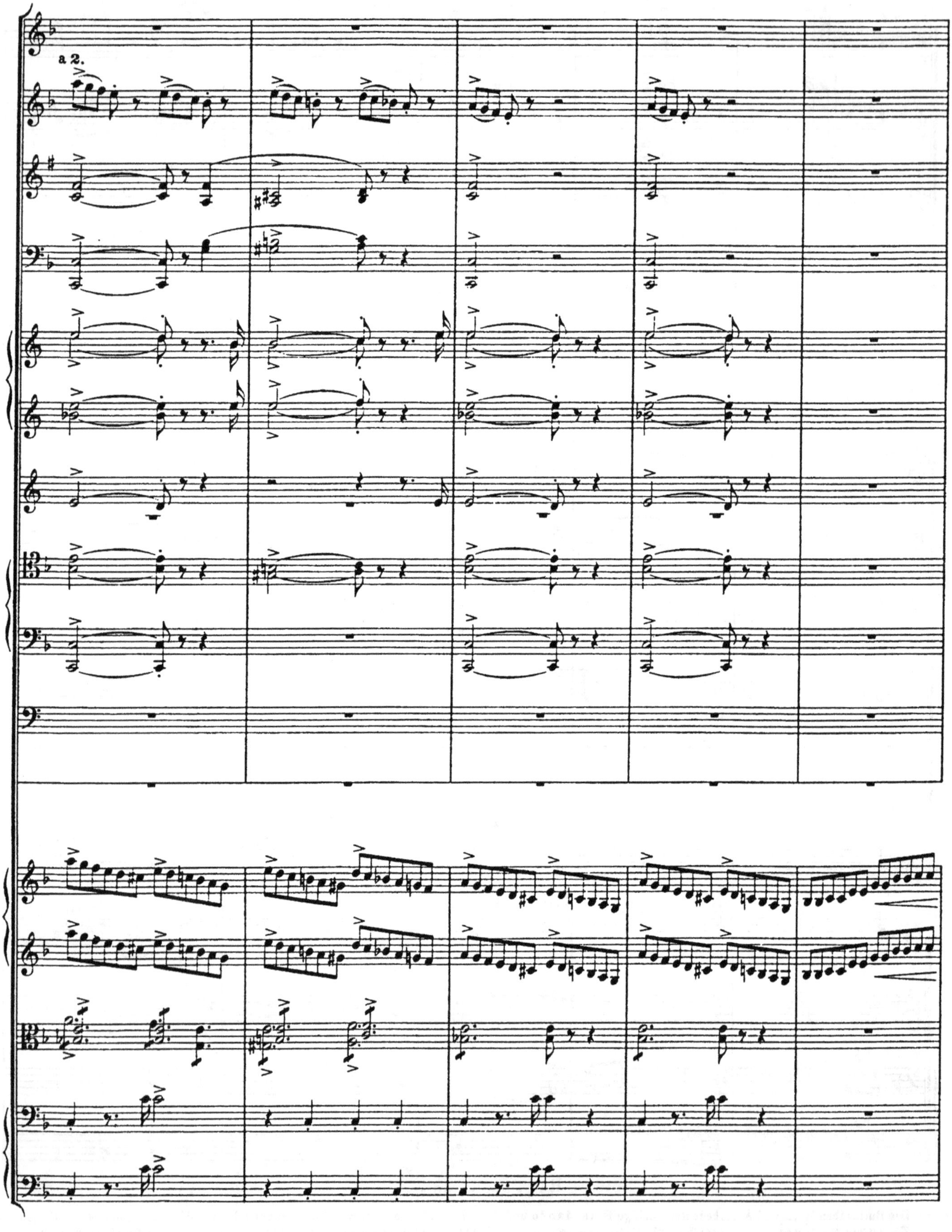
a 2.

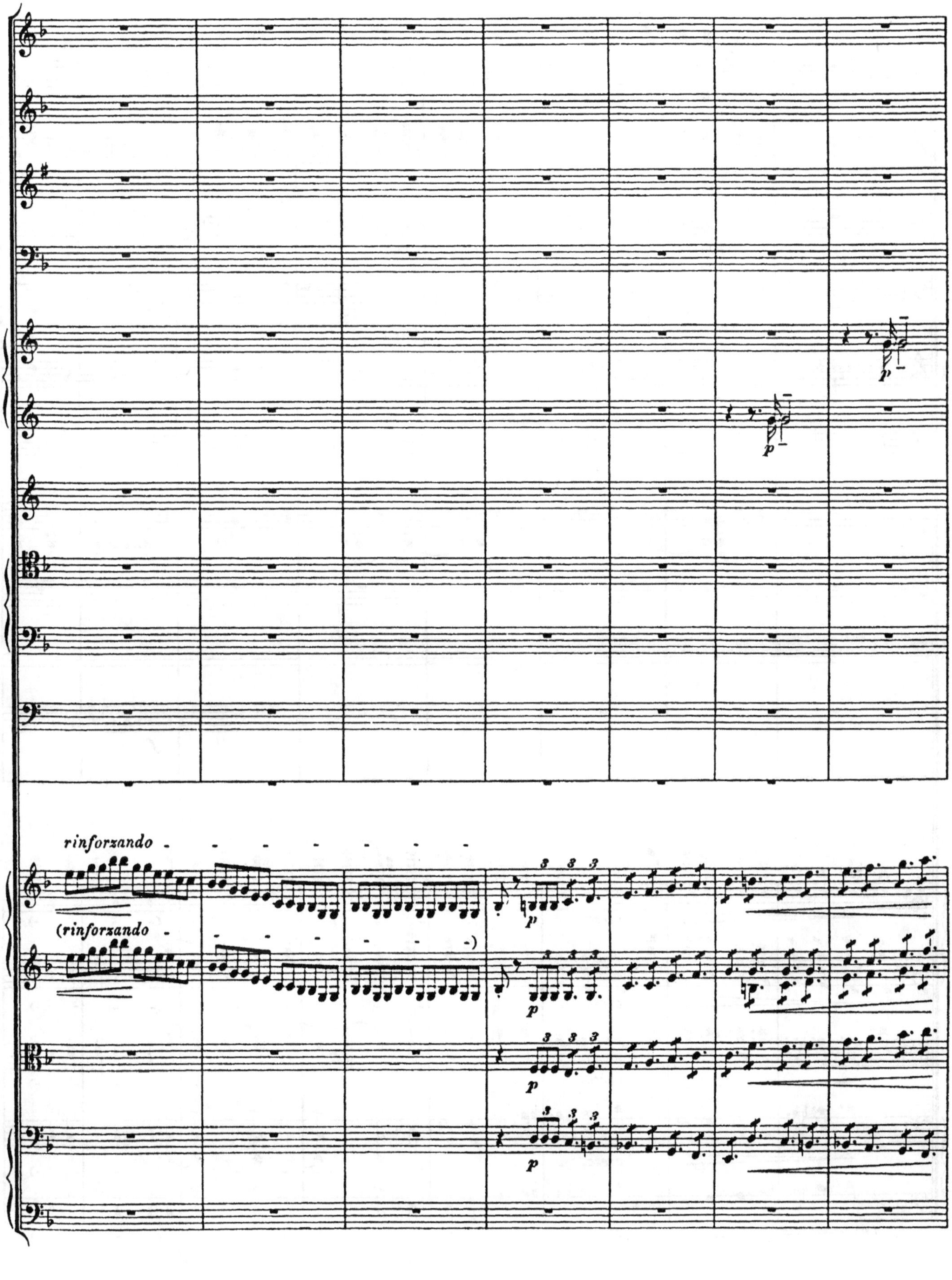
rinforzando
(rinforzando
3
p

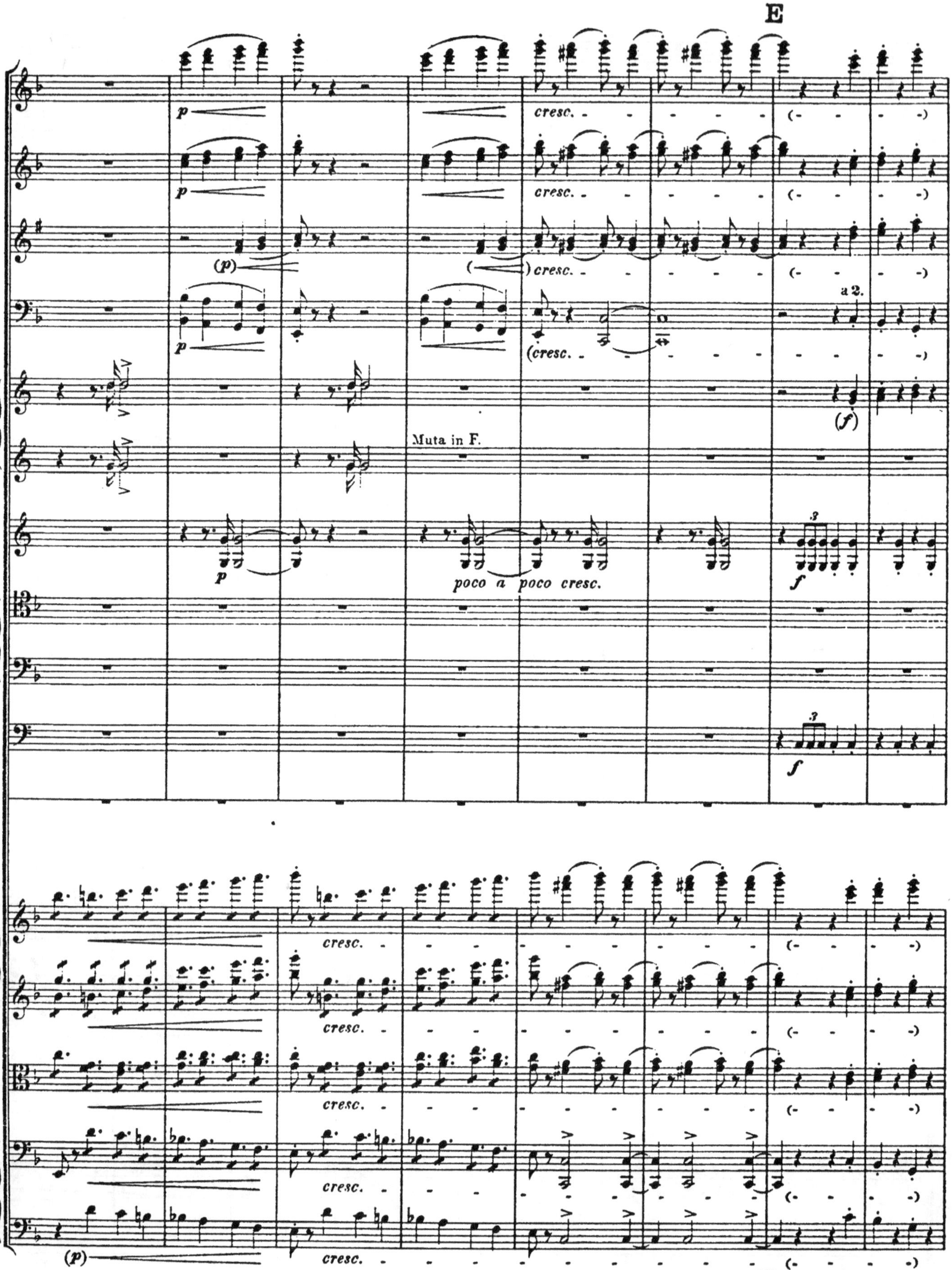
E
p
cresc.
(p)
(cresc.
a 2.
(f)
Muta in F.
poco a poco cresc.
f
3
E

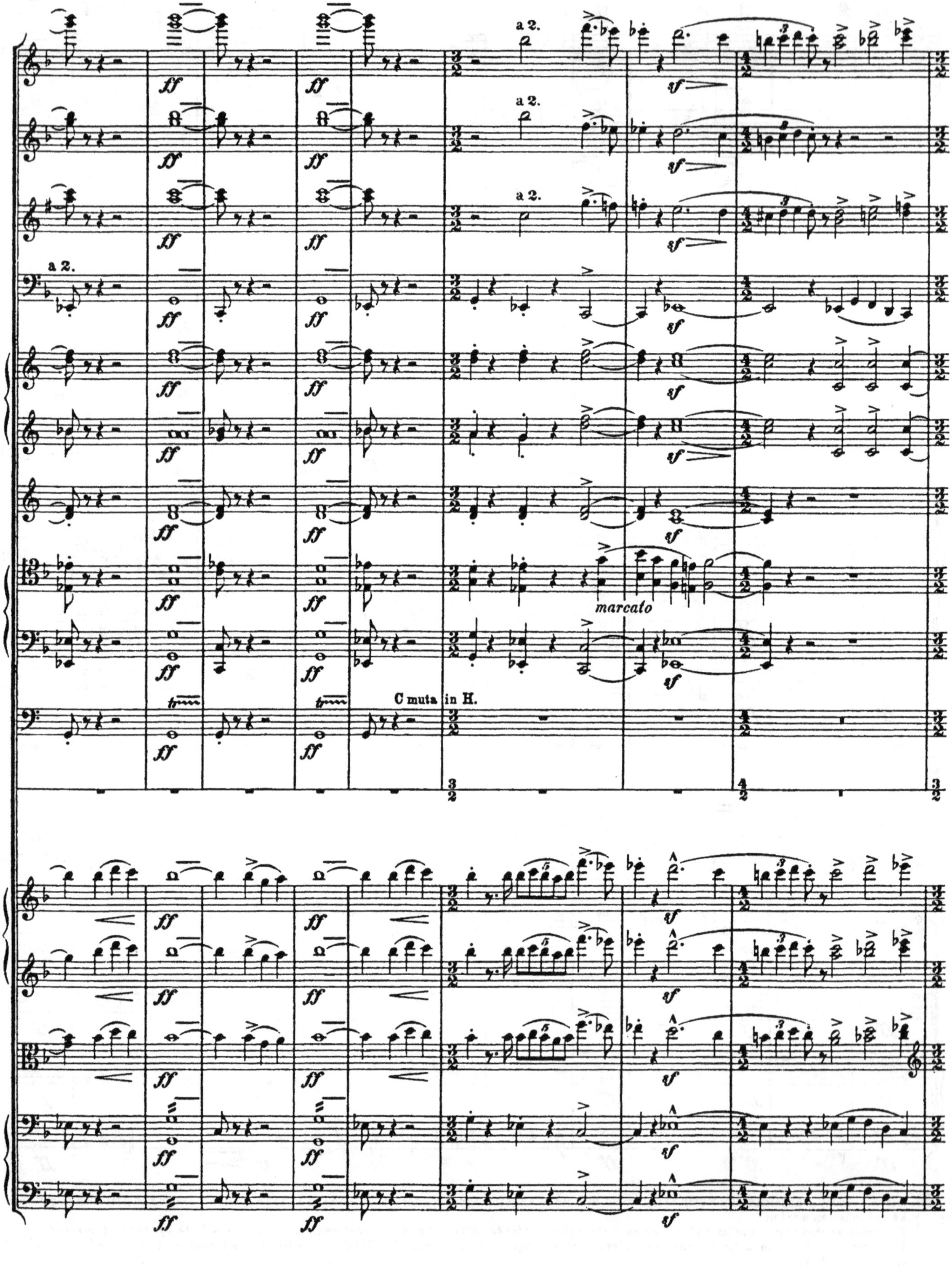
a 2.
marcato
C muta in H.

F
(p) dolce espress.
(p) dolce espress.
(p) dolce espress.
a 2.
(p) dolce espress.
dim.
dim.
con grazia
dim.
(p) dolce
(p) dolce con grazia
(p) dolce
(p)
F

p
p
(II. p)
con grazia
(p)
(p)
(II. p)
con grazia
dolce espress.
con grazia
dolce espress.
dolce espress.
dolce espress.

con grazia
espress.
dim.
Solo.
(II. p)
espress.
p
espress.
p
espress.
(p)
Solo.
(p) espress.
div.
dolce espress.
p
dolce espress.
p
dolce espress.
Solo.
(p)
dolce espress.

poco rall.
(p)
dim.-smorz.
(I. p)
p
(II. p)
muta in C.
(p) dim.-smorz.
dolce
dolce smorz.
p
poco rall.

G
smorz.
div.
p tranquillo
div.
p tranquillo
(p) molto espressivo
pizz.
G (p)

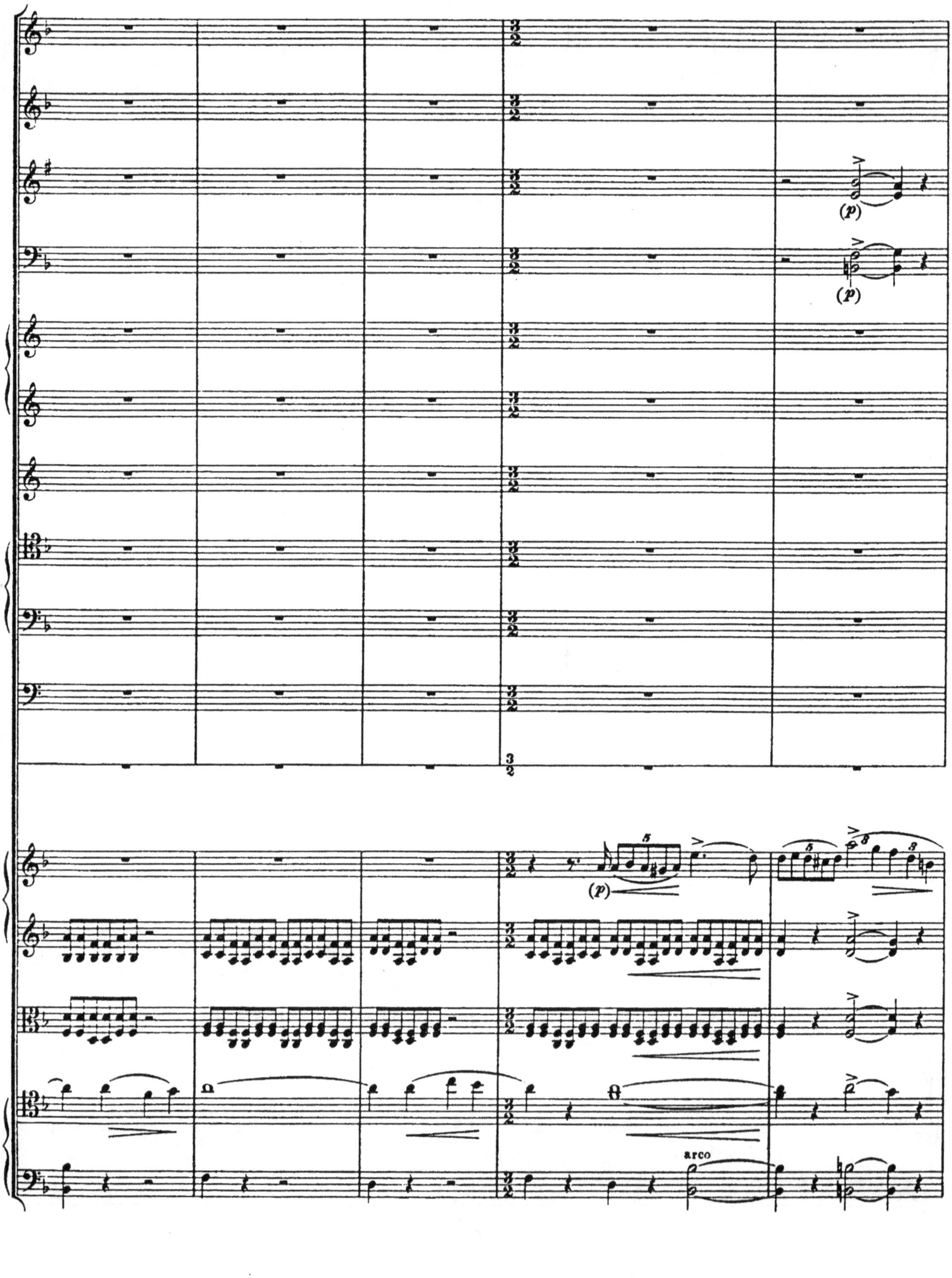
(p)
(p)
(p)
arco

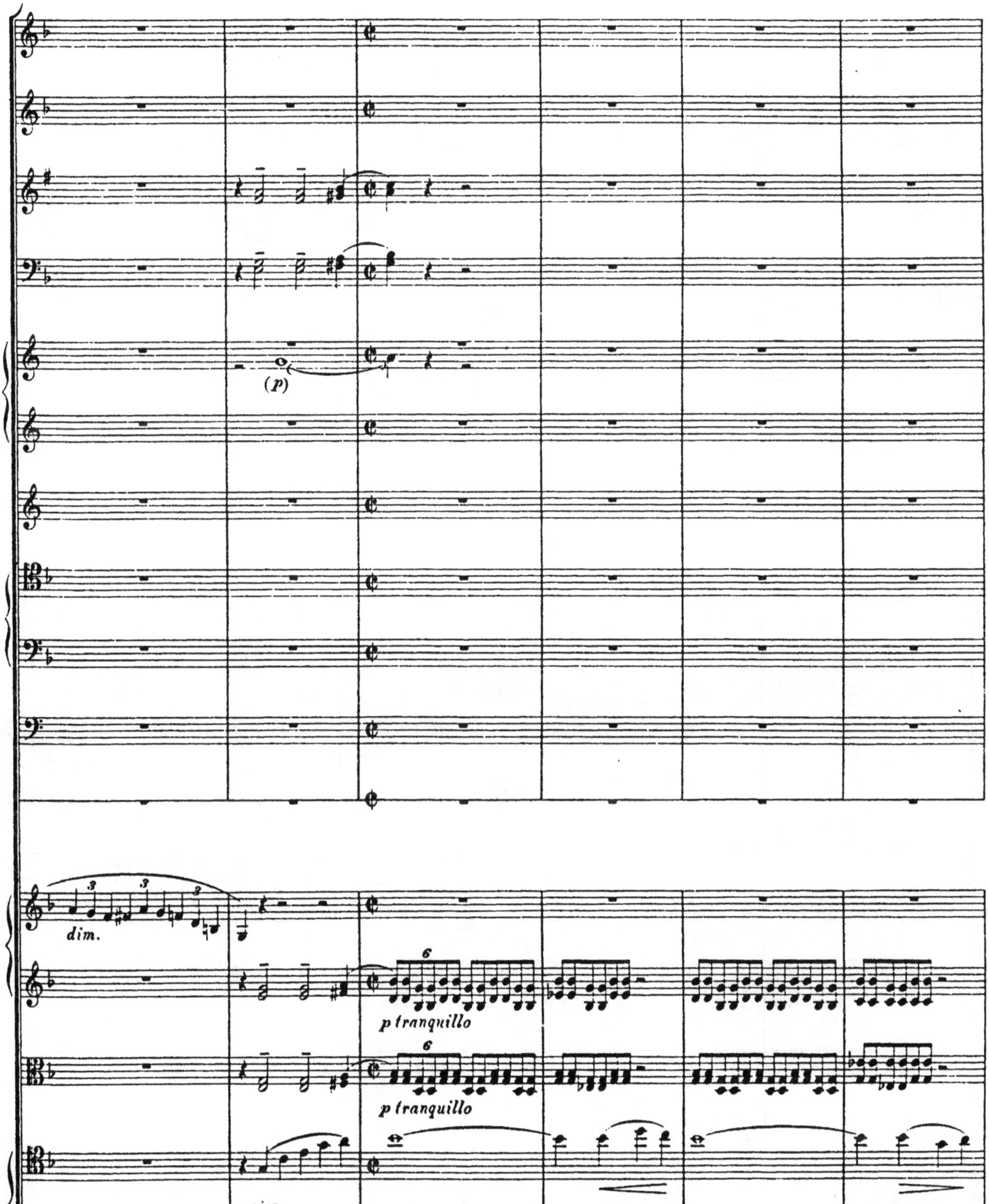
(p)
dim.
p tranquillo
p tranquillo
pizz.

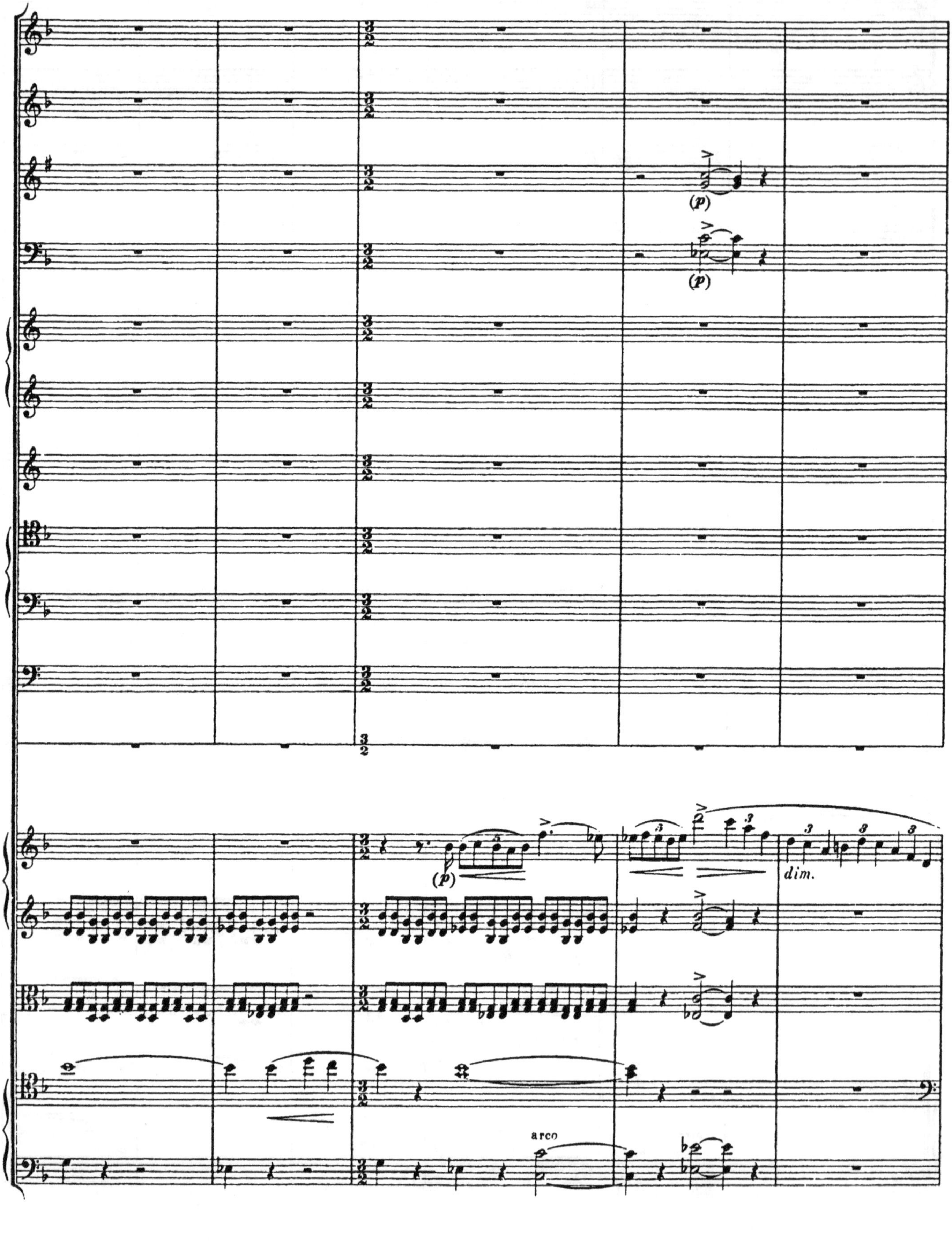
(p)
(p)
(p)
dim.
arco

(p) dolce
p
sempre tranquillo
dolce
dolce
p
sempre tranquillo
dolce
sempre tranquillo e dolce
sempre tranquillo e dolce
pizz.
arco
semplice
arco
ten.
pizz.
ten.

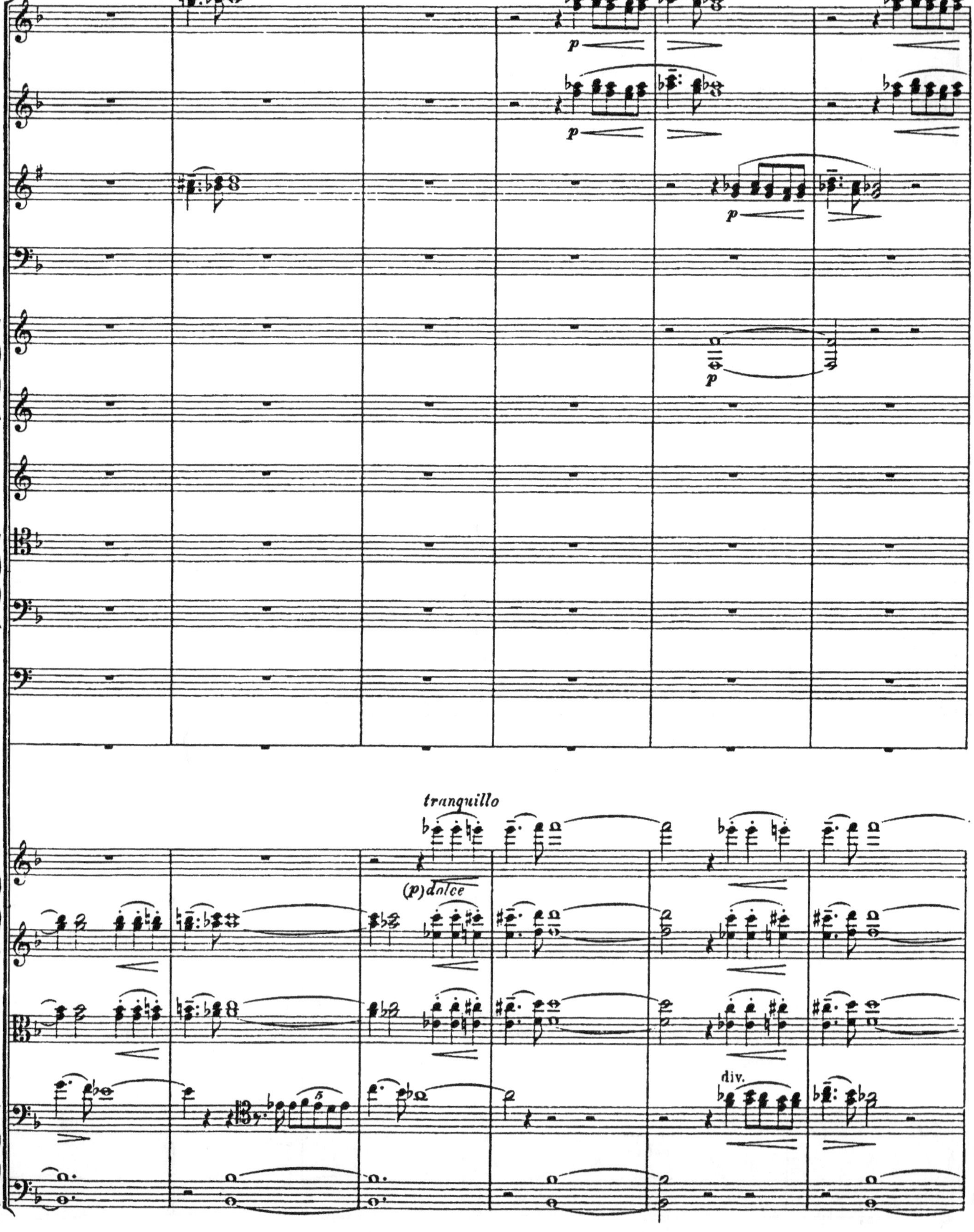
p
p
p
p
tranquillo
(p) dolce
div.

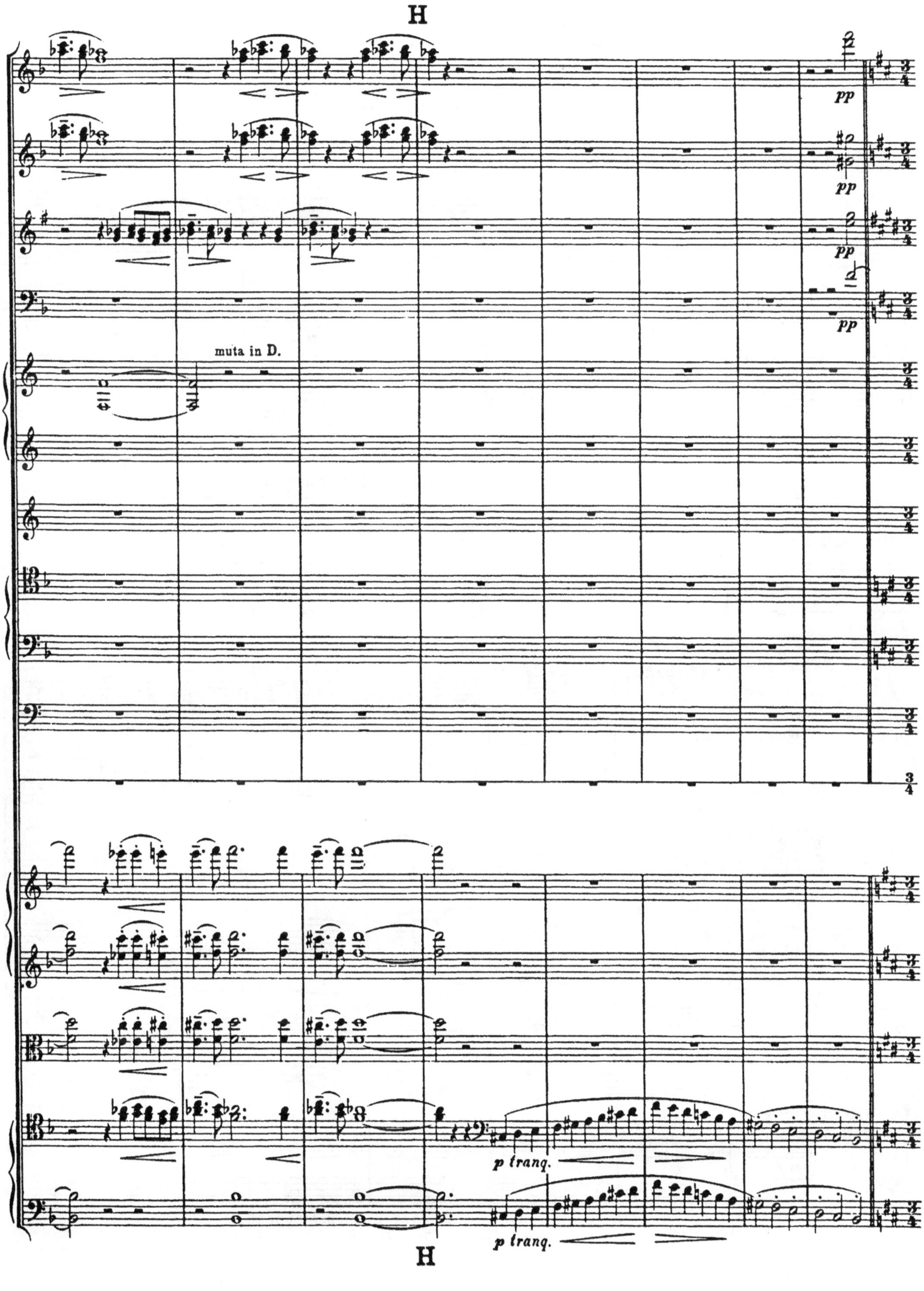
H
pp
pp
pp
pp
muta in D.
p tranq.
p tranq.
H

Da lebte mir der Baum, die Rose,
Mir sang der Quellen Silberfall,
Es fühlte selbst das Seelenlose
Von meines Lebens Widerhall.

The rose was ever on me smiling
Then, how the silv'ry waterfall
Would sing to me in strains beguiling.
My life re-echoed over all.

Alors vivaient pour moi les arbres et les roses,
La source me chantait son harmonieux chant,
Alors je confondais les arbres et les choses
Qui tressaillaient de vie à mon souffle puissant.

Quieto e sostenuto assai. **(Die ♩ wie früher die ♪) aber nicht schleppend.**
(♩ come ♪ prima) ma non trascinando.

Quieto e sostenuto assai. **(Die ♩ wie früher die ♪) aber nicht schleppend.**
(♩ come ♪ prima) ma non trascinando.

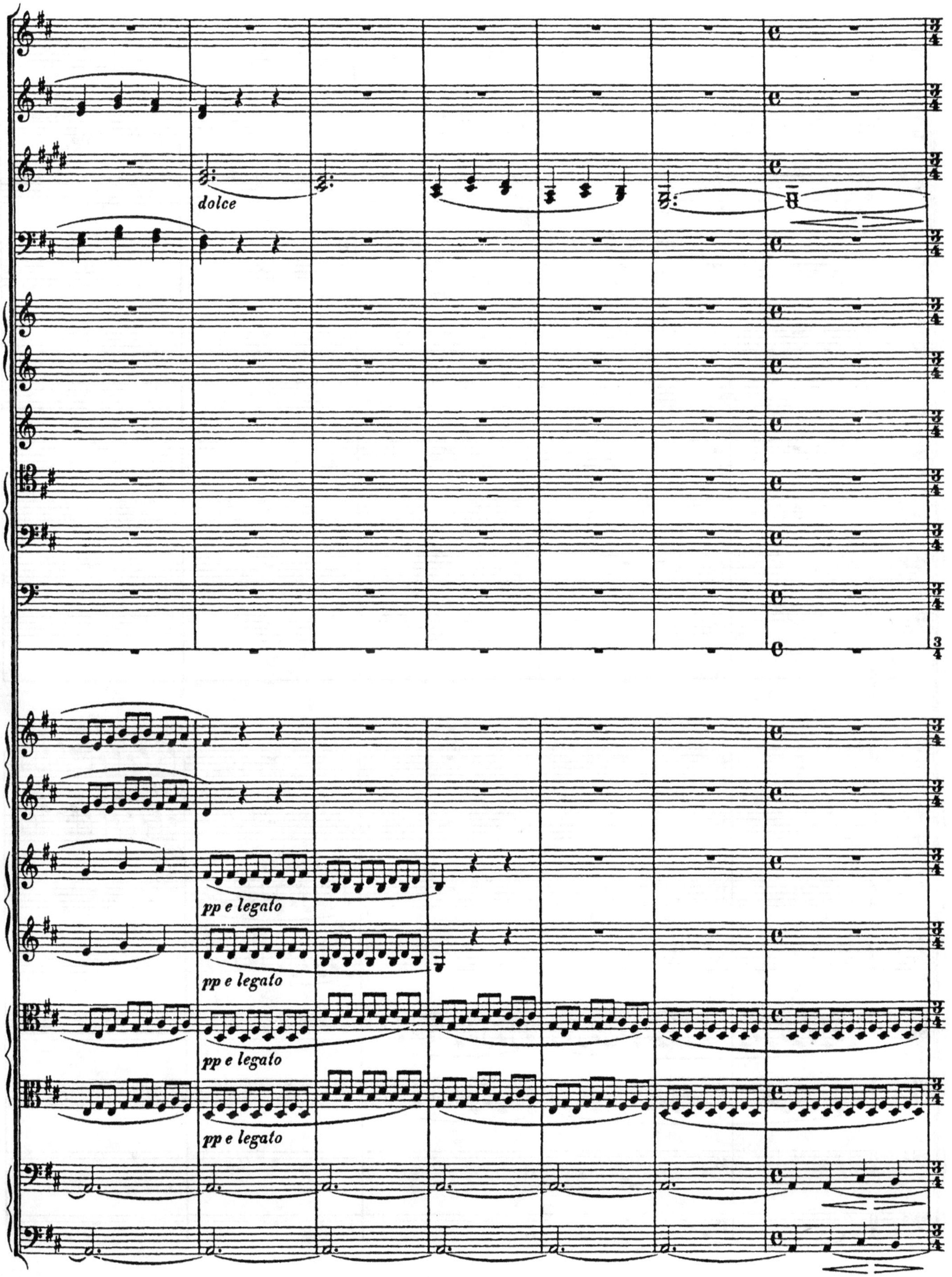
dolce
pp e legato
pp e legato
pp e legato
pp e legato

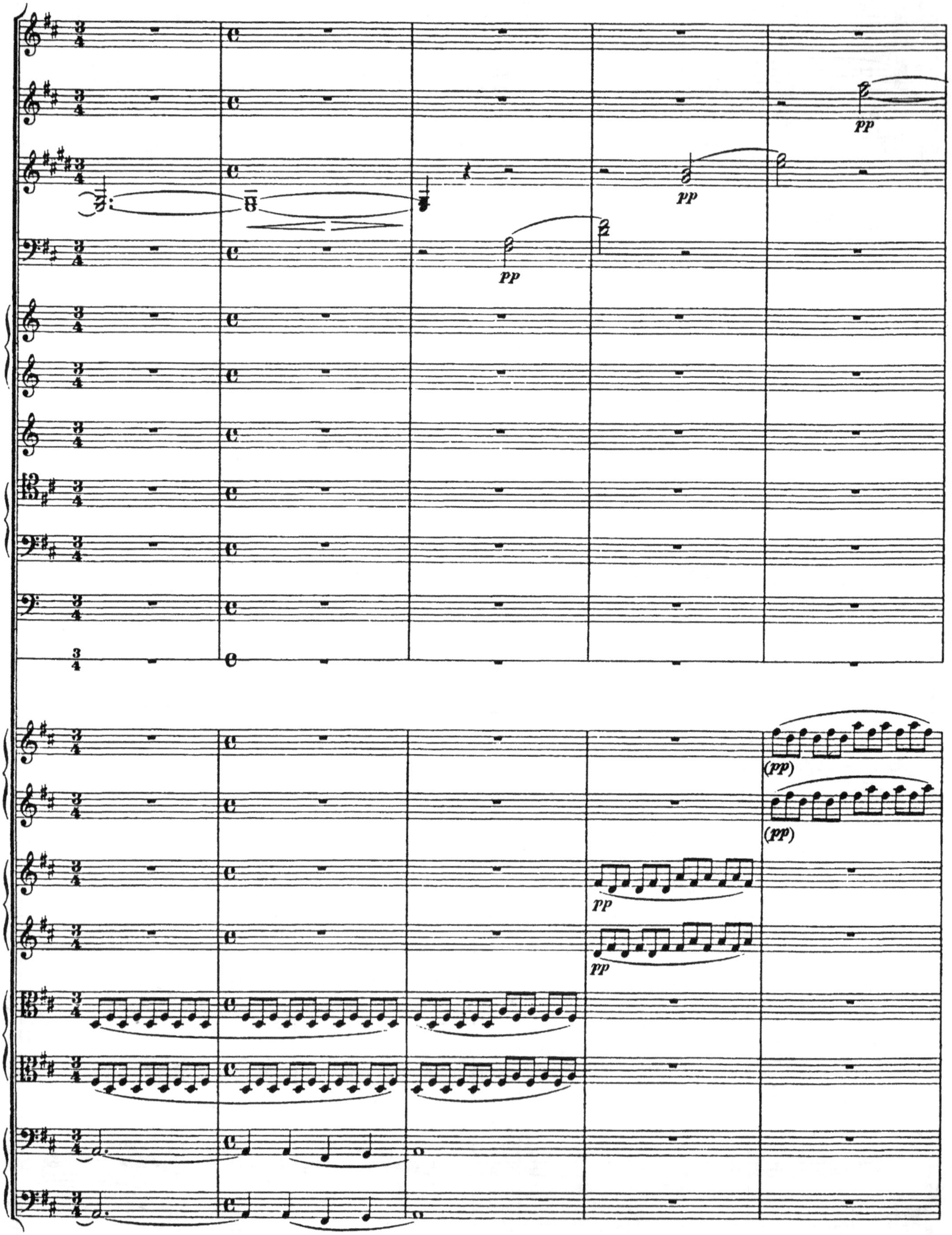
pp
pp
pp
(pp)
(pp)
pp
pp

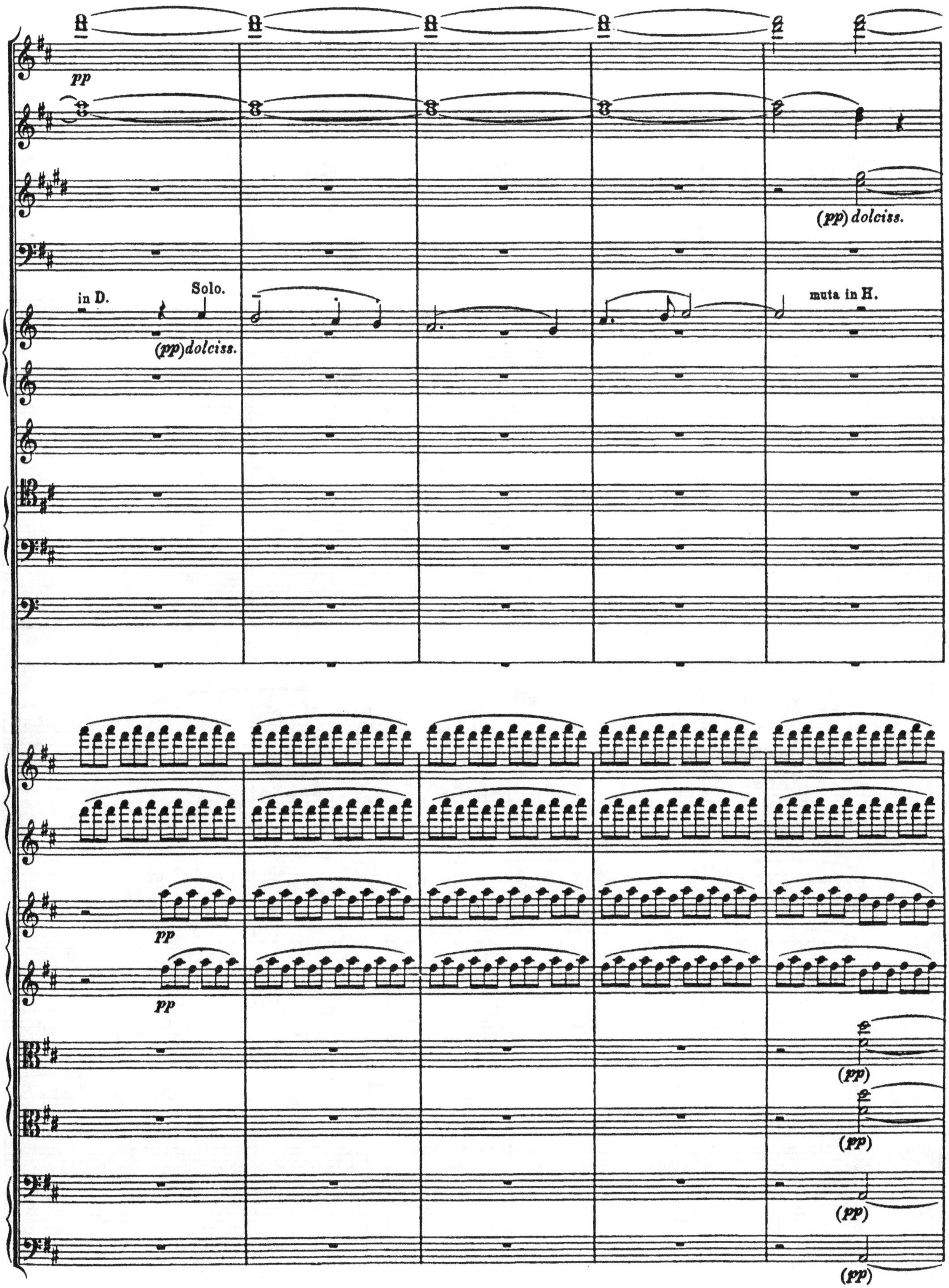
pp
(pp) dolciss.
in D.
Solo.
(pp)dolciss.
muta in H.
pp
pp
(pp)
(pp)
(pp)
(pp)

I
dolciss.
dolciss.
dolciss.
pp sempre dolciss. e legato
pp sempre dolciss. e legato
pp sempre dolciss. e legato
pp sempre dolciss. e legato
pp
pp
pp
pp
I

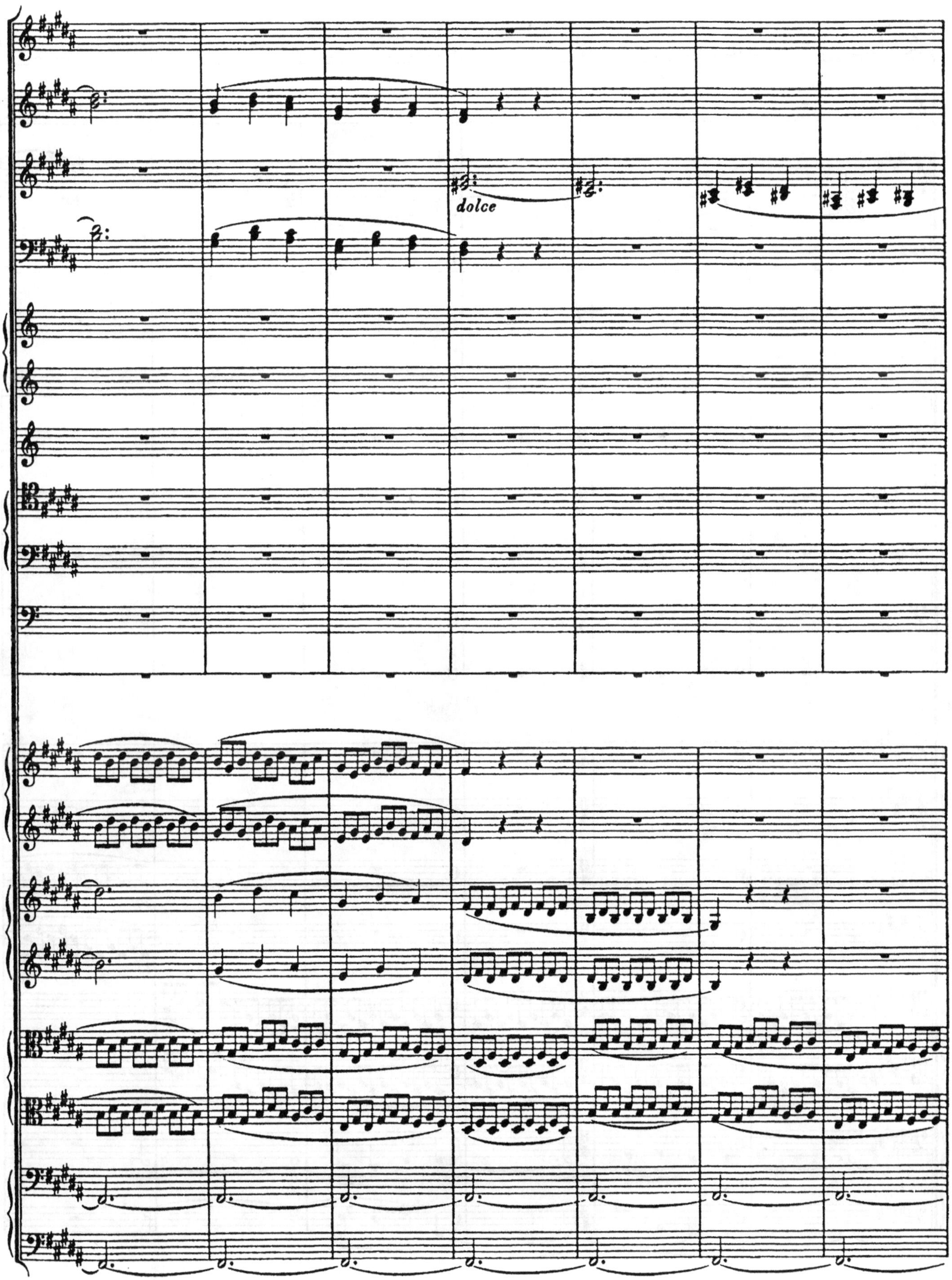
dolce

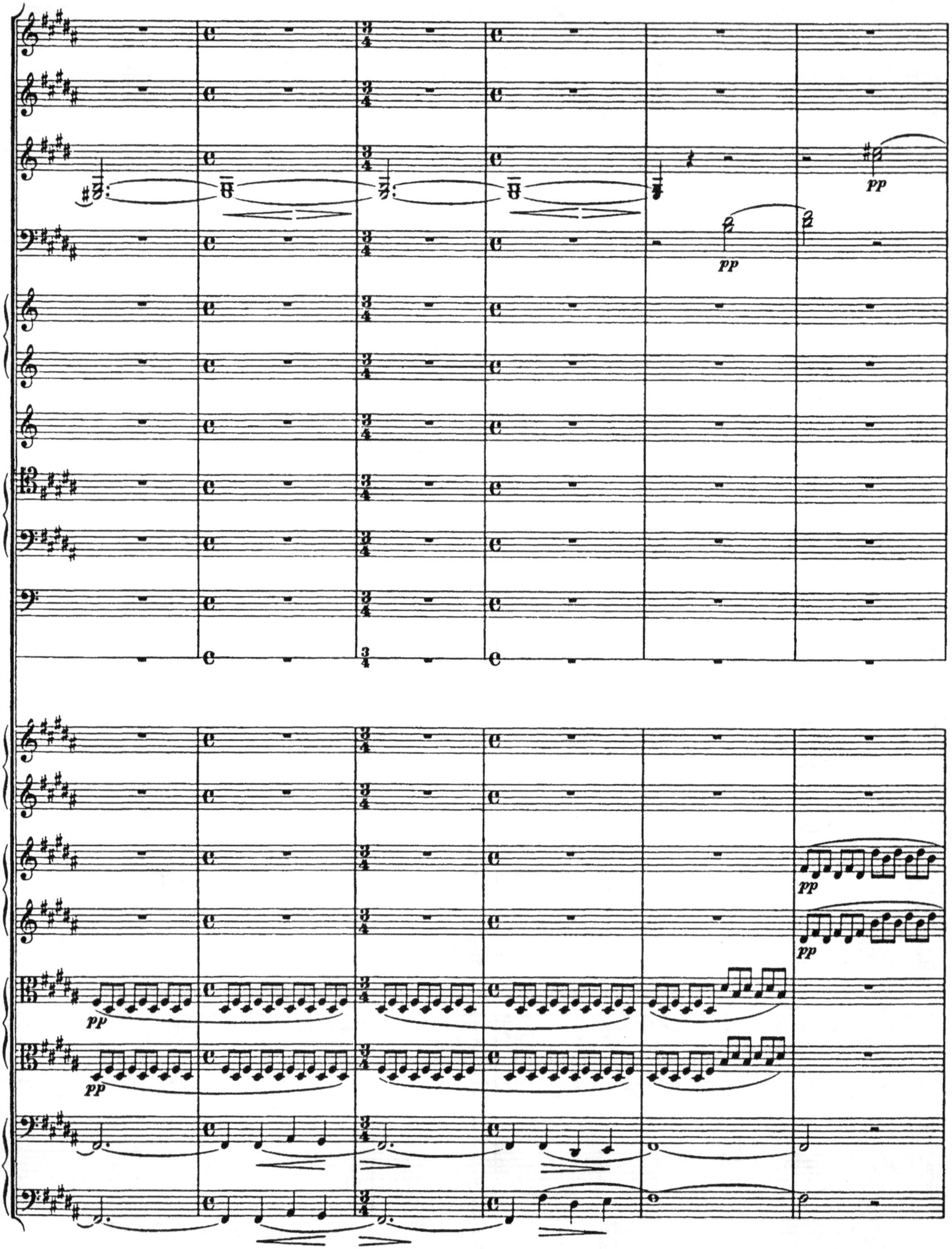
pp
pp
pp
pp
pp
pp

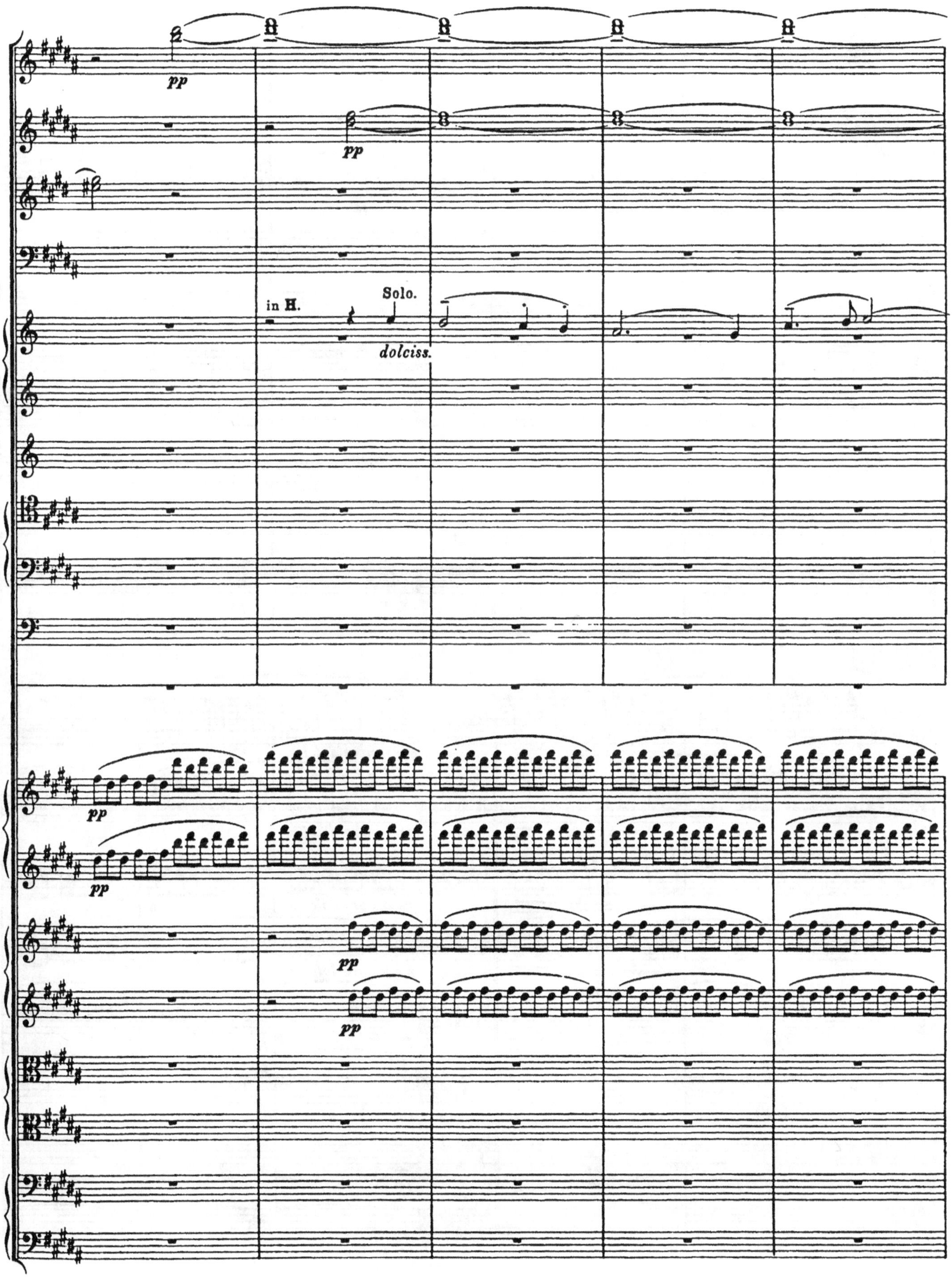
pp
pp
in H.
Solo.
dolciss.
pp
pp
pp
pp

dolciss.
sempre dolciss.
dolciss.
muta in C.
tr
ppp
pp sempre dolciss.
pp sempre dolciss.
pp sempre dolciss.
pp sempre dolciss.
(pp)
pp
(pp)
pp
(pp)
pp
(pp)
pp

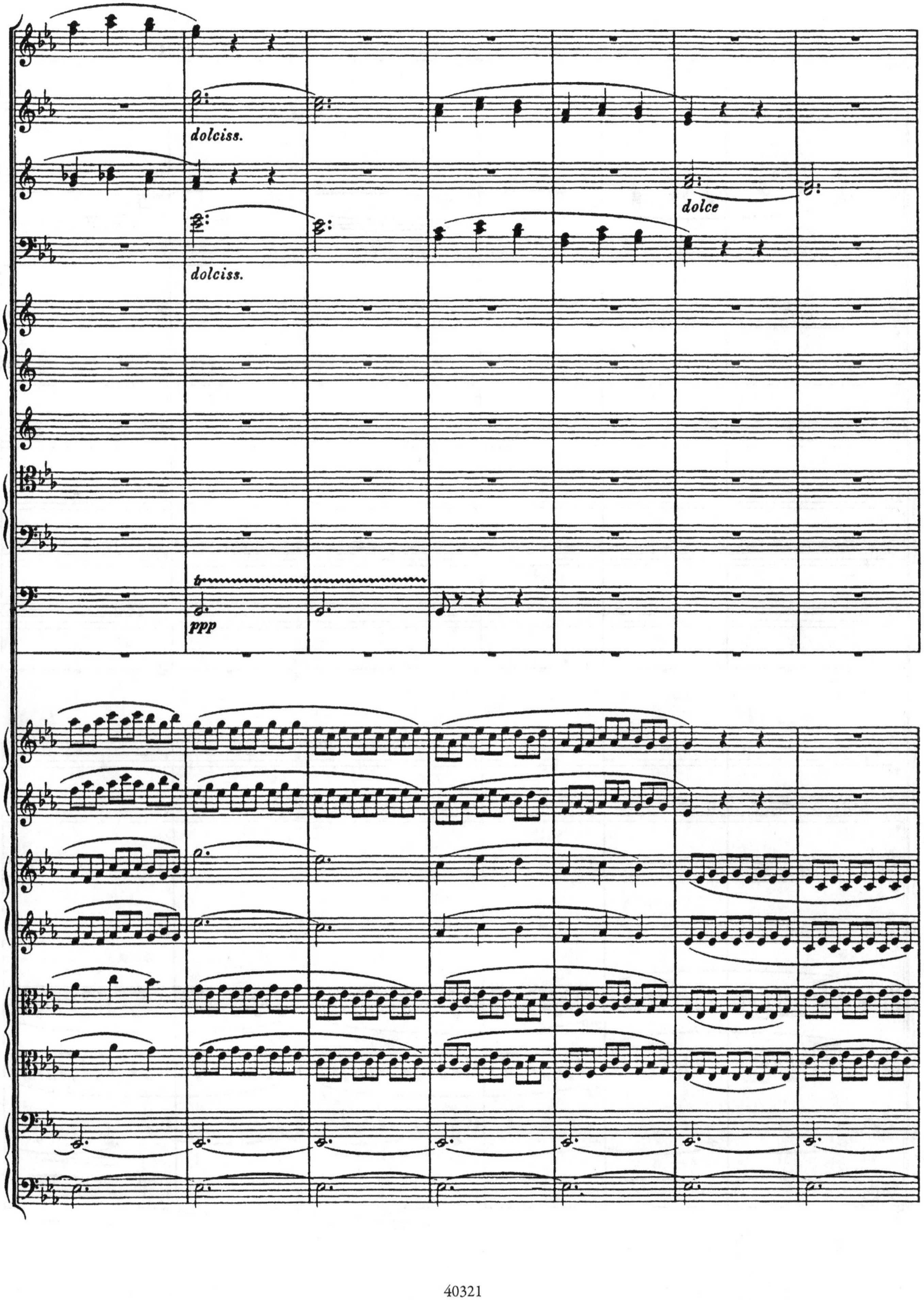
dolciss.
dolce
dolciss.
tr
ppp

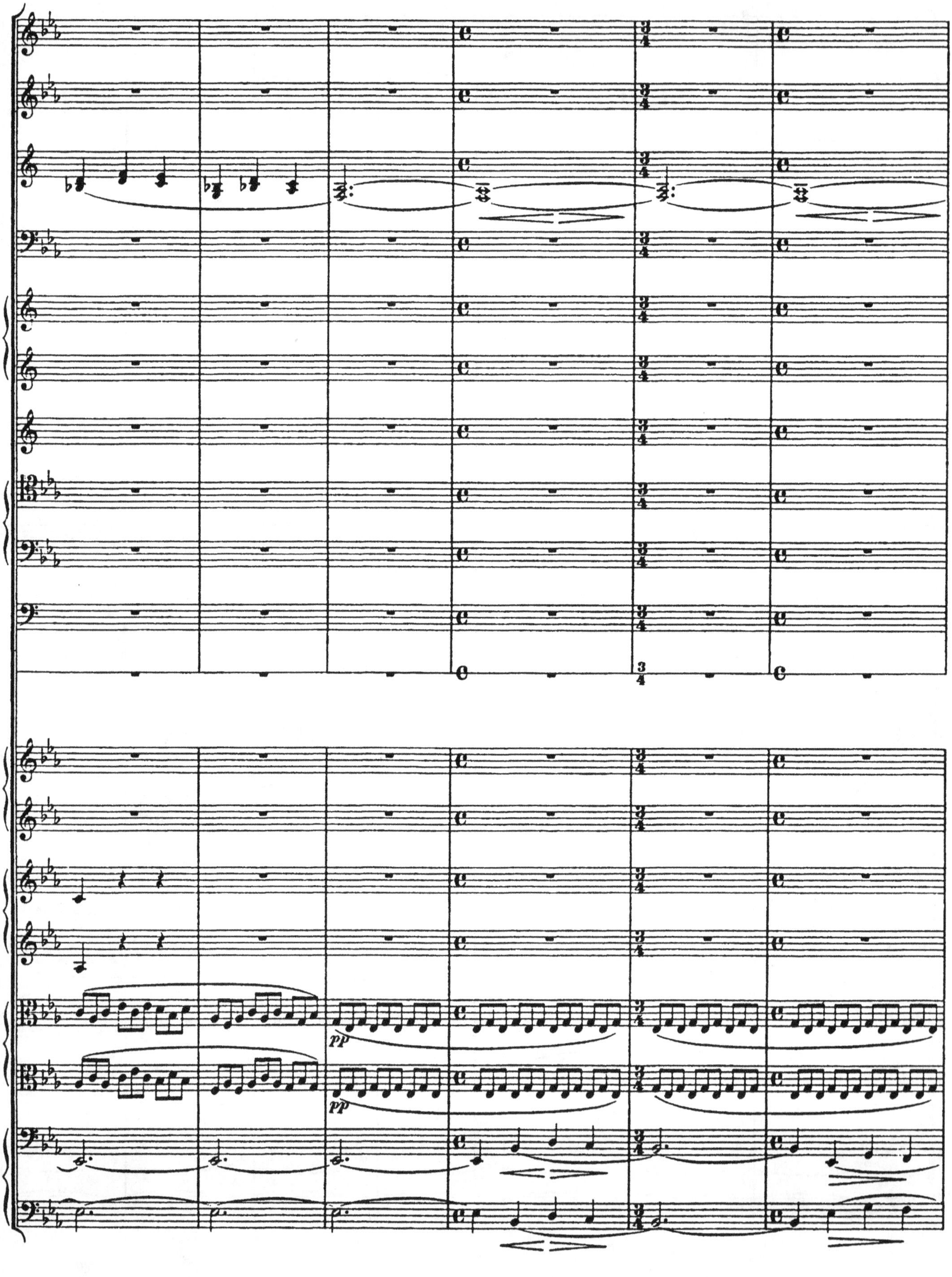
pp
pp

Wie einst mit flehendem Verlangen
Pygmalion den Stein umschloss,
Bis in des Marmors kalte Wangen
Empfindung glühend sich ergoss:
So schlang ich mich mit Liebesarmen
Um die Natur, mit Jugendlust,
Bis sie zu atmen, zu erwarmen
Begann an meiner Dichterbrust.

As once with longings deep, impassioned,
Pygmalion the marble clasped
Until the cold form he had fashioned
At last with breath responsive gasped:
So also I, who fondly loved her.
Fair Nature in mine arms once pressed
Until my glowing heart had moved her
To warm hers on my poet's breast.

Comme Pygmalion de sa lèvre brûlante
Embrassait autrefois la pierre avec ardeur
Jusqu'à ce que le corps de la statue amante
Répondant à l'amour, s'échauffât sur son cœur;
De même, je pressais sur mon cœur de poète
La divine nature; elle, à ma passion
S'animait, à ma voix ne restait pas muette,
Et semblait consacrer notre intime union.

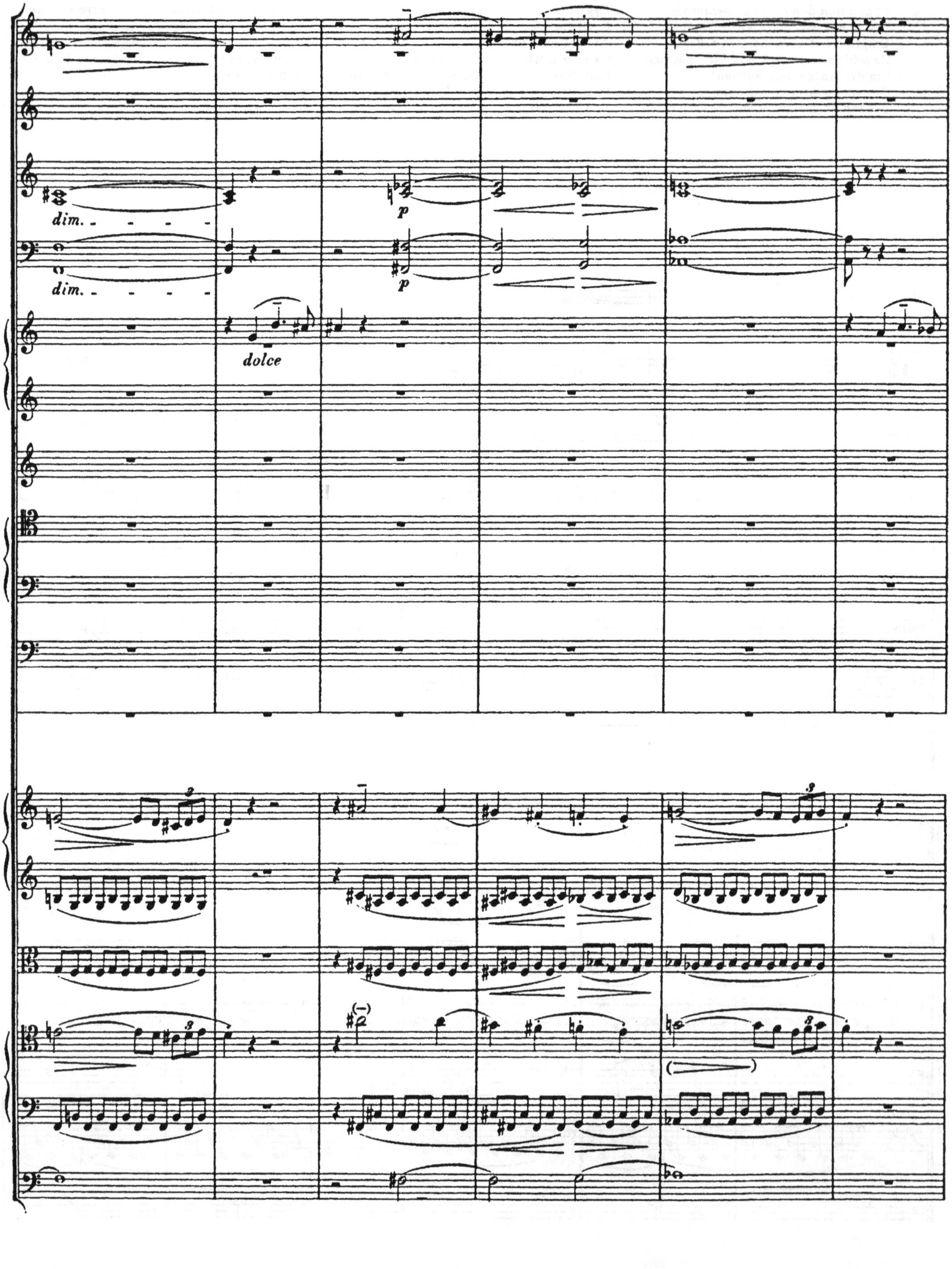
dim.
dim.
p
p
dolce

(p) dolce, espressivo   cresc.

Von hier an bis zu dem Buchstaben L „*Allegro molto mosso*" allmählich accelerando.
Poco a poco accelerando sin alla lettera **L**.

Von hier an bis zu dem Buchstaben L „*Allegro molto mosso*" allmählich accelerando.
Poco a poco accelerando sin alla lettera **L**.

K
a 2.
rinforzando
a 2.
rinforzando
rinforzando
(rinforzando)
rinforzando
rinforzando
IV. muta in F.
p sempre molto espress.
(p) espressivo
pp
pp
pp
rinforzando
(rinforzando)
rinforzando
(rinforzando)
rinforzando
p sempre molto espress.
p sempre molto espress.
p sempre molto espress.
K

(II. p)
III. muta in F.
(IV.) in F.
(p espr.)
sempre piano
(p)
sempre piano
sempre piano

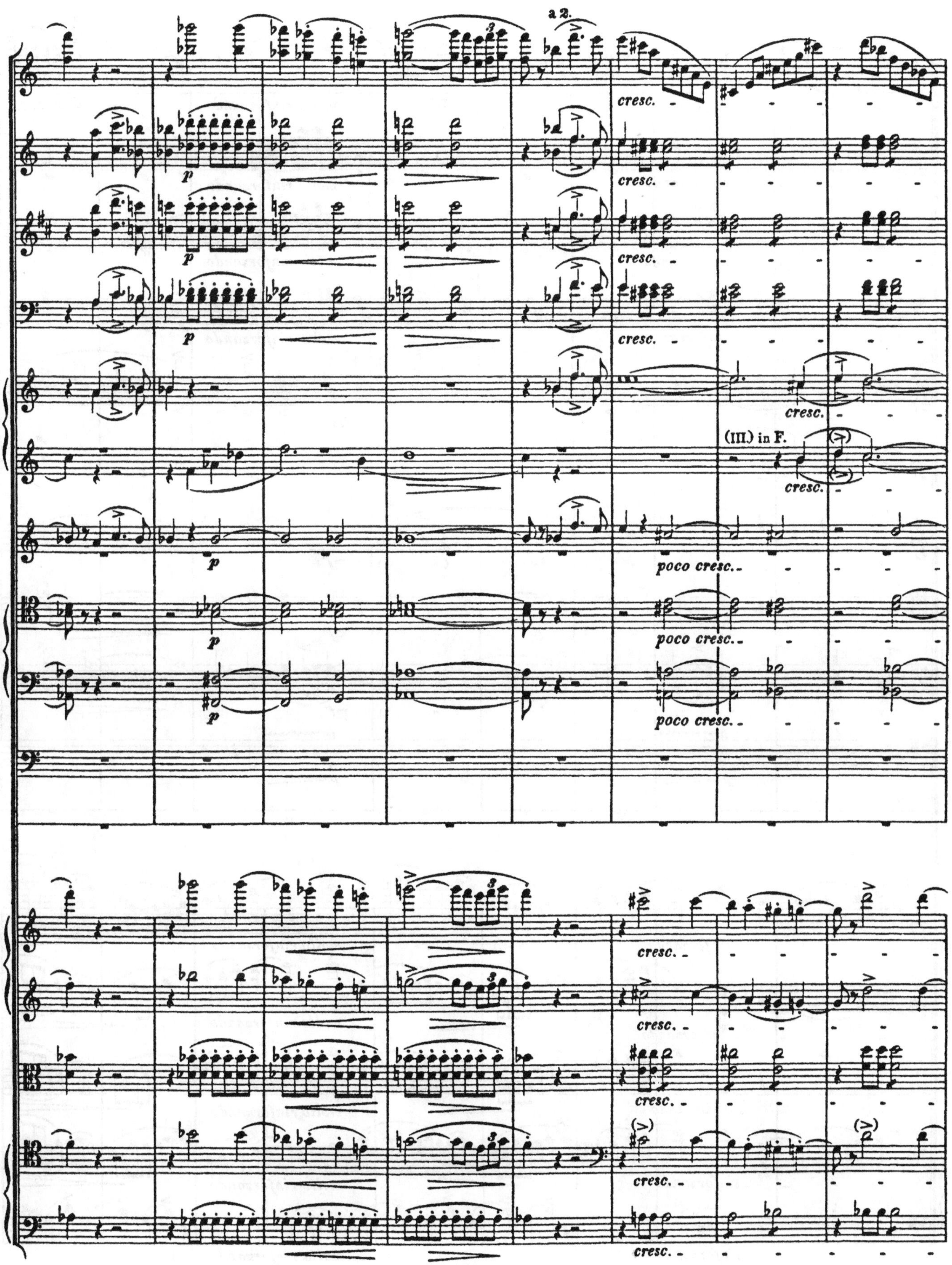
a 2.
cresc.
p
(III) in F.
poco cresc.

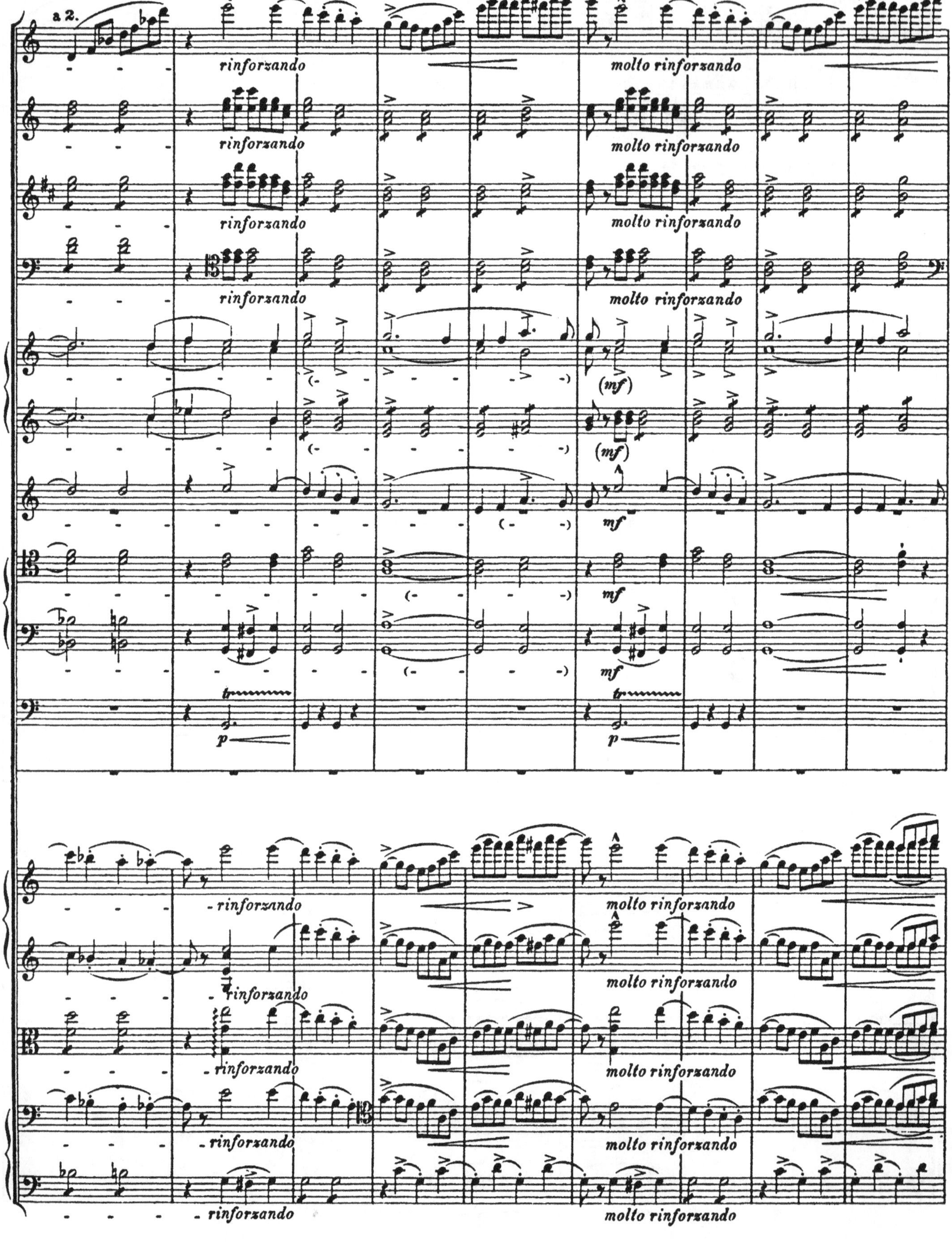
a 2.
rinforzando
molto rinforzando
(mf)
mf
p
tr

Allegro molto mosso.

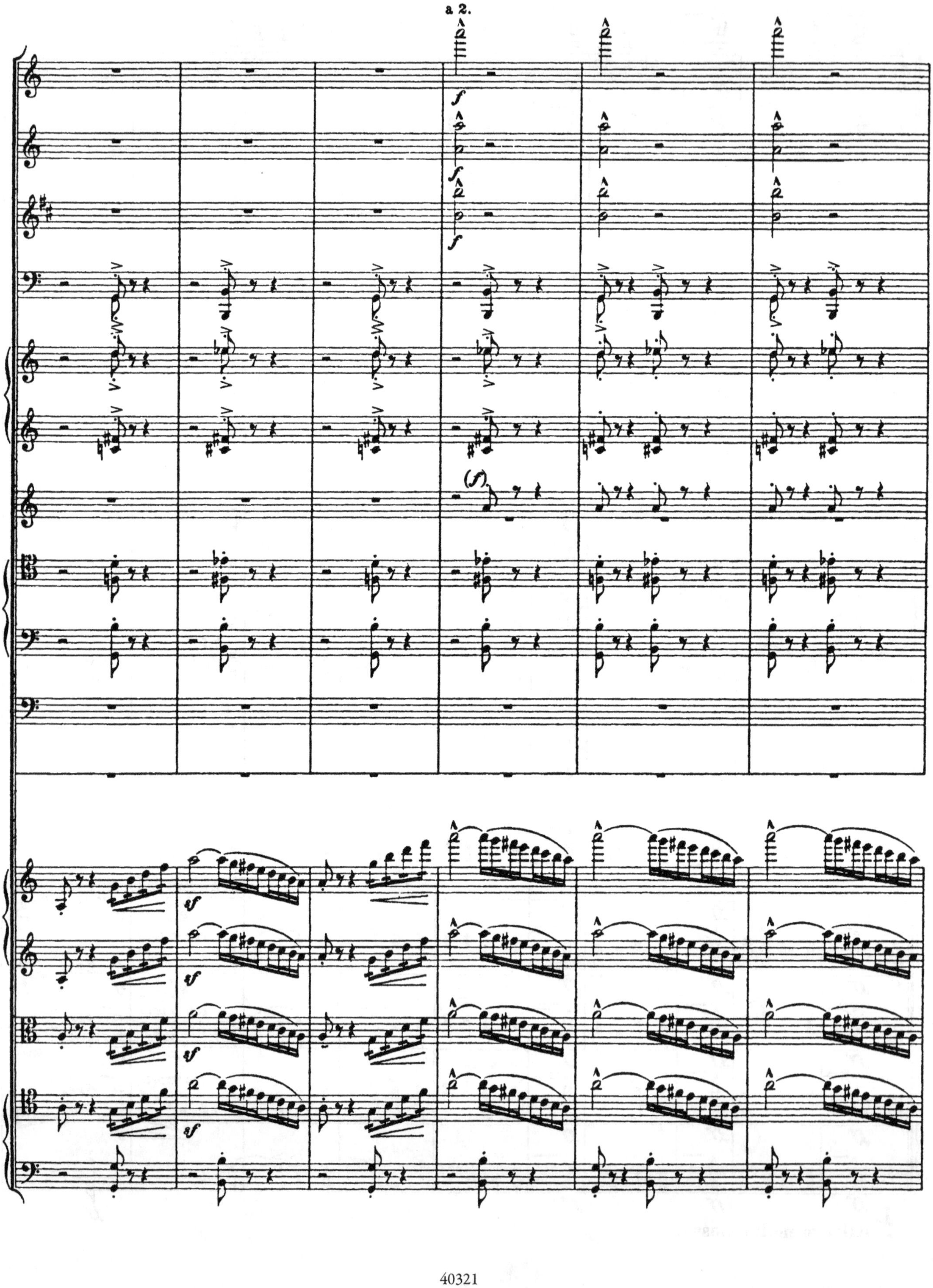
a 2.
f
f
f
(f)
sf
sf
sf
sf

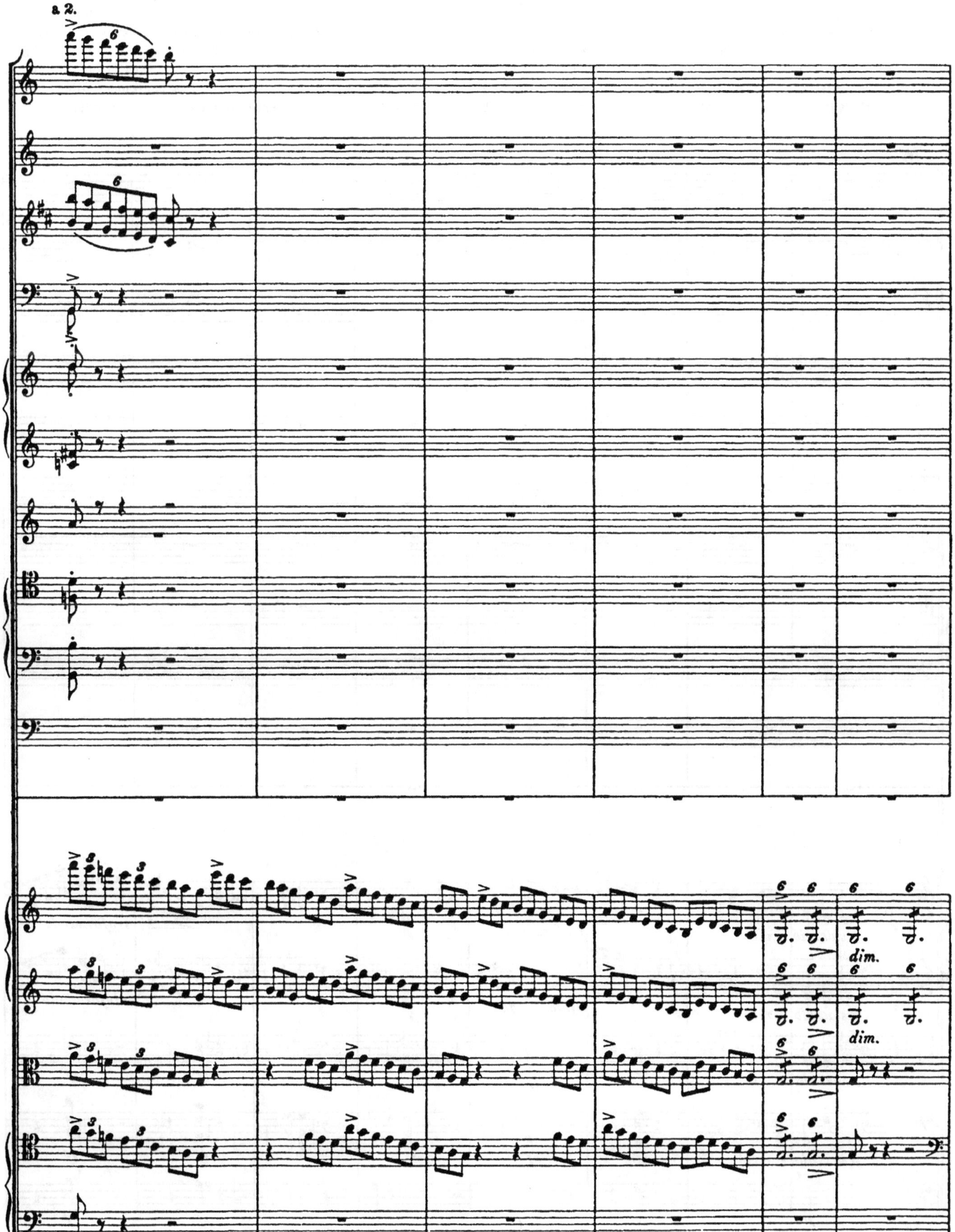
a 2.
dim.
dim.

Wie tanzte vor des Lebens Wagen	Ah! then how danced before Life's chariot	Et de ma jeune vie ô le riant cortège,
Die luftige Begleitung her:	The unsubstantial company!	Allègre compagnon de mes pensers joyeux:
Die Liebe mit dem süssen Lohue,	There Love appeared with gifts enchanting,	C'étaient le tendre amour et son doux privilège,
Das Glück mit seinem goldnen Kranz,	And Fortune with her golden crown,	Le bonheur qui promet d'exaucer tous nos vœux,
Der Ruhm mit seiner Sternenkrone,	Nor was Fame's star-gemmed crown e'en wanting—	Et la gloire portant sa couronne étoilée,
Die Wahrheit in der Sonne Glanz!	Round Truth his mantle Sol had thrown.	Et la vérité sainte en toute sa clarté.

accelerando
p vivo
p vivo
a 2.
(p) marcato
scherzando
p leggiero
p
leggiero
p
leggiero
p
sf
sf
leggiero
p
sf
sf
leggiero
(p)
sf
sf
arco
accelerando
leggiero

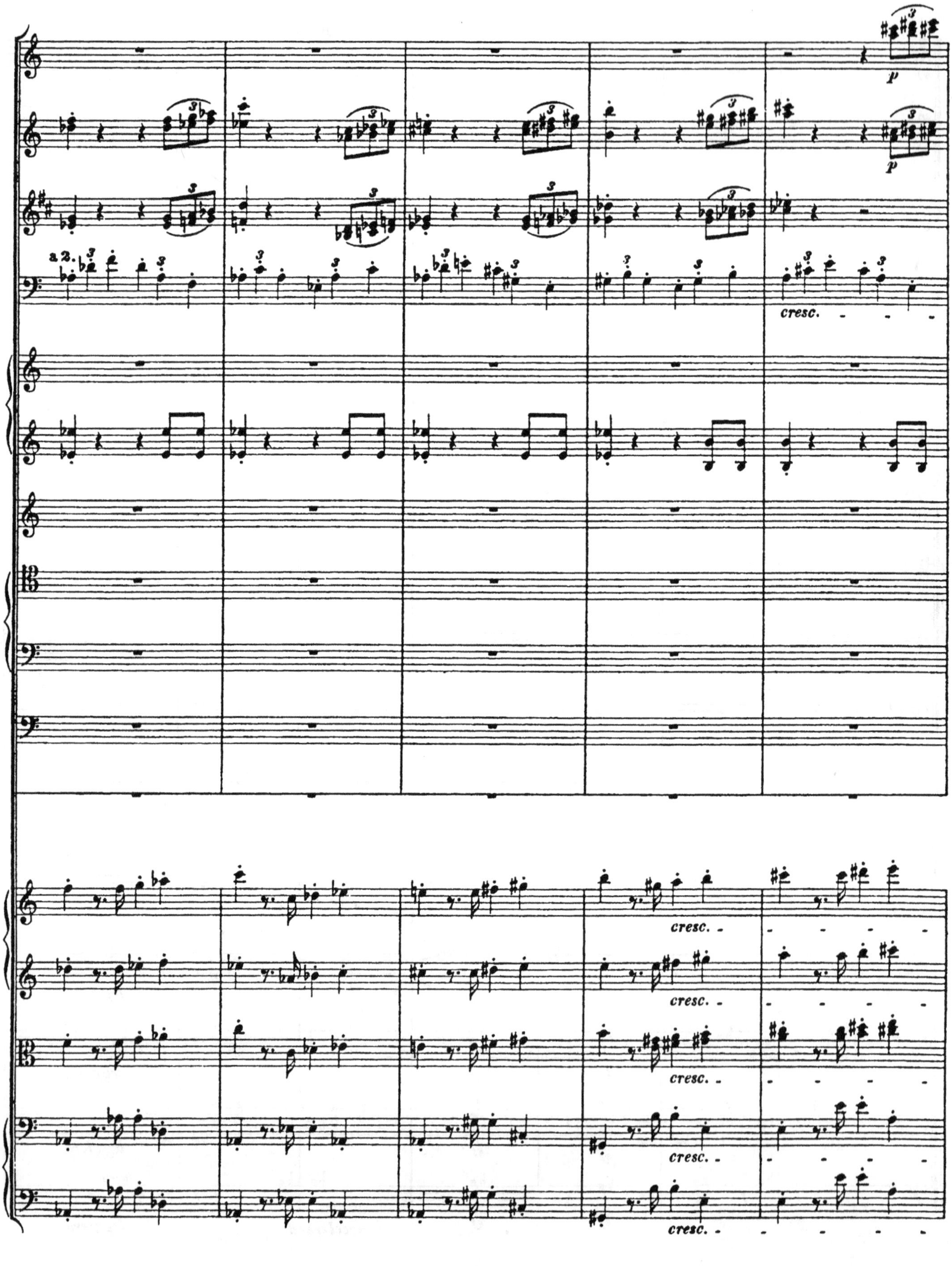
a 2.
p
p
cresc.
cresc.
cresc.
cresc.
cresc.
cresc.

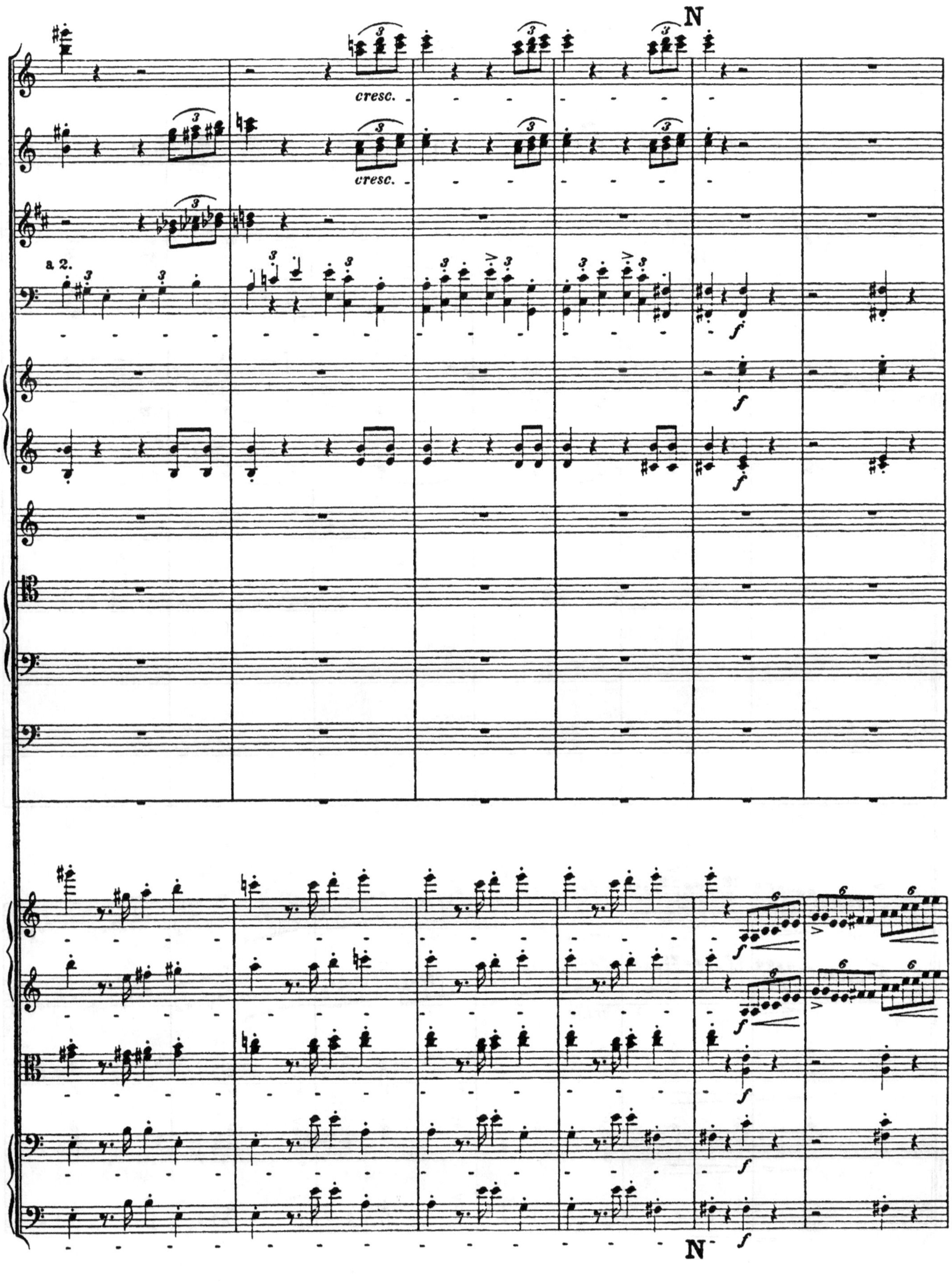
N
cresc.
cresc.
a 2.
f
f
f
f
f
f
f
f
N

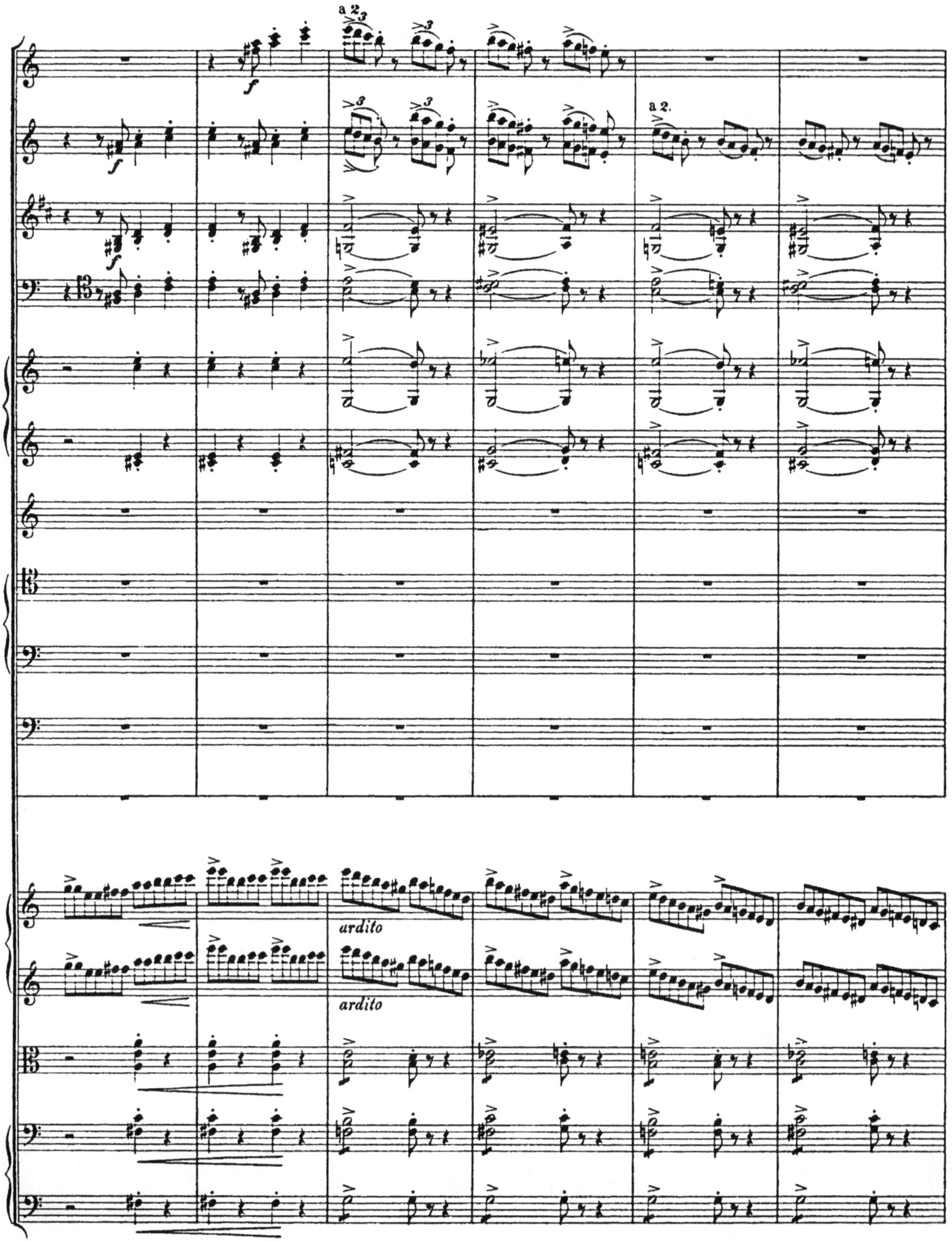
a 2
f
f
f
a 2.
ardito
ardito

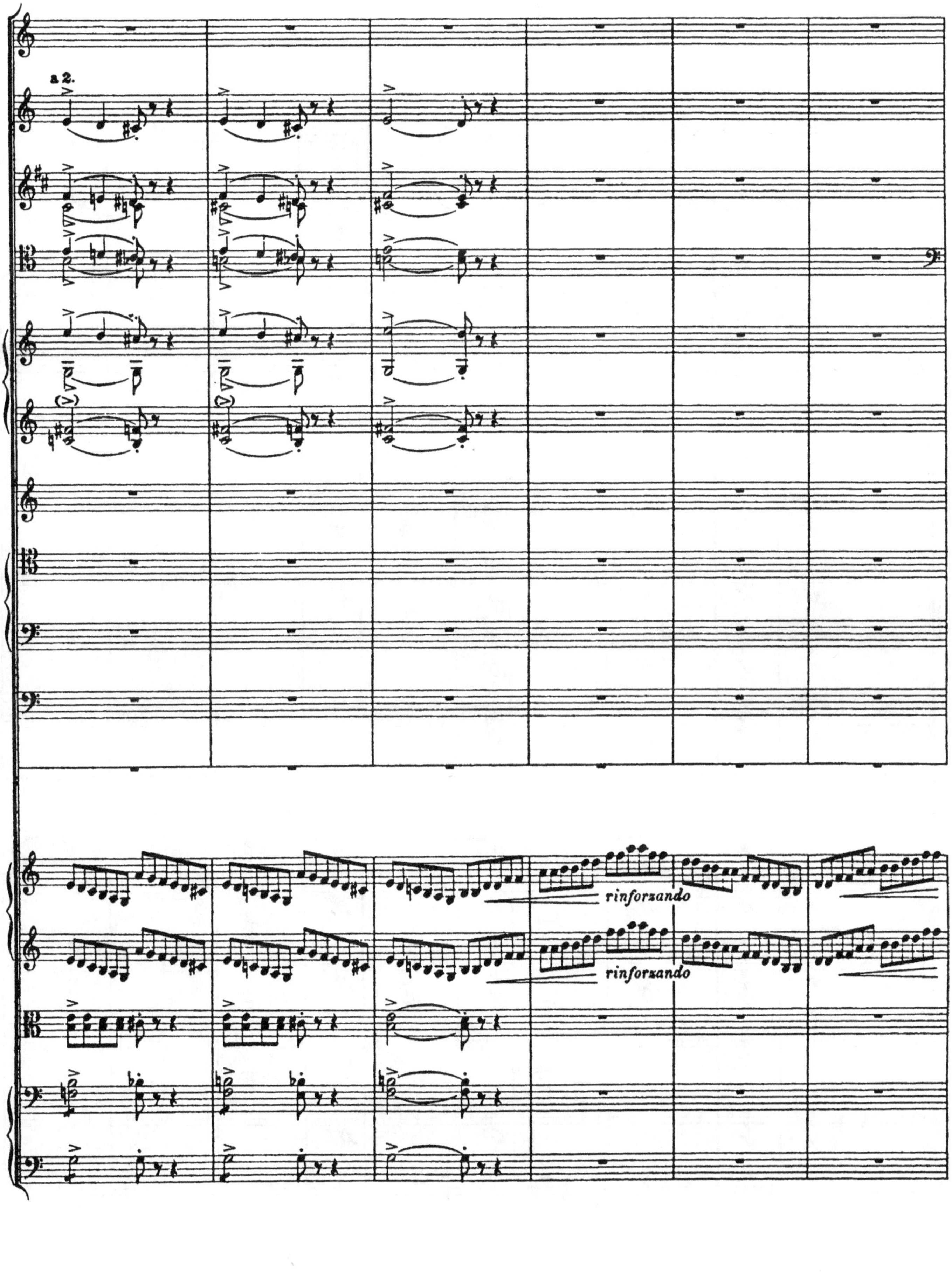
a 2.
rinforzando
rinforzando

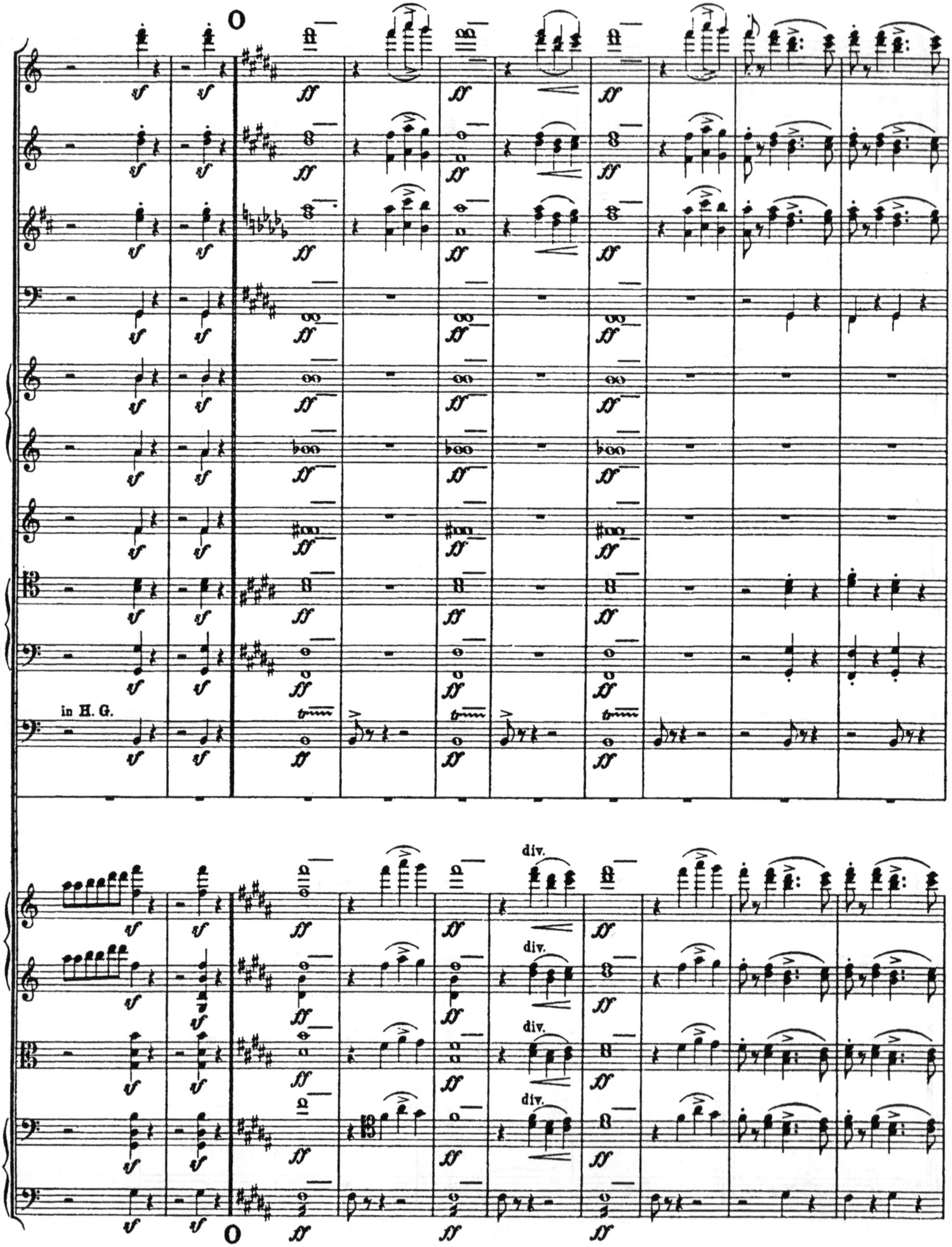
O
in H. G.
div.
div.
div.
div.
O

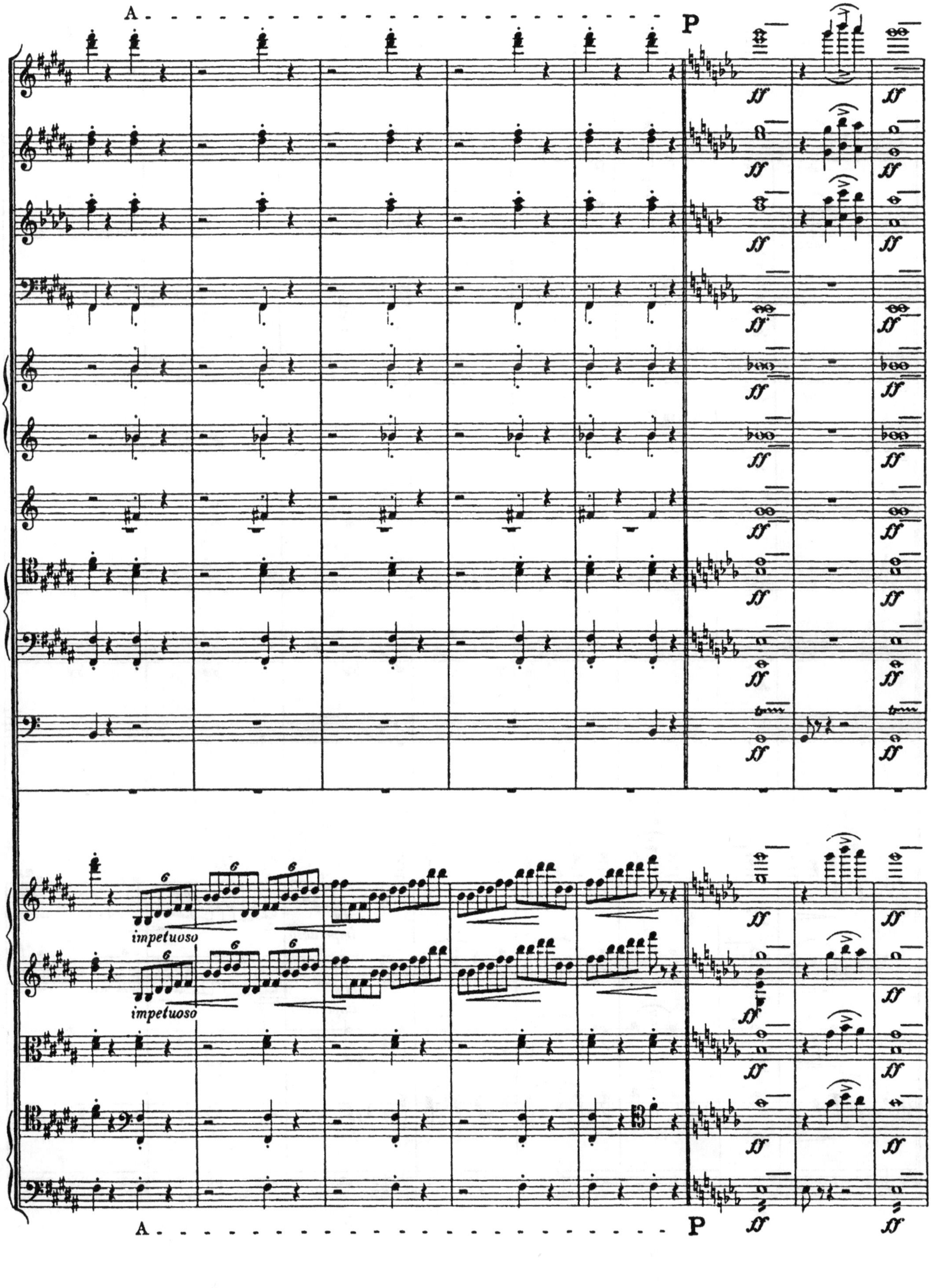
A
P
ff
6
impetuoso
impetuoso
A
P

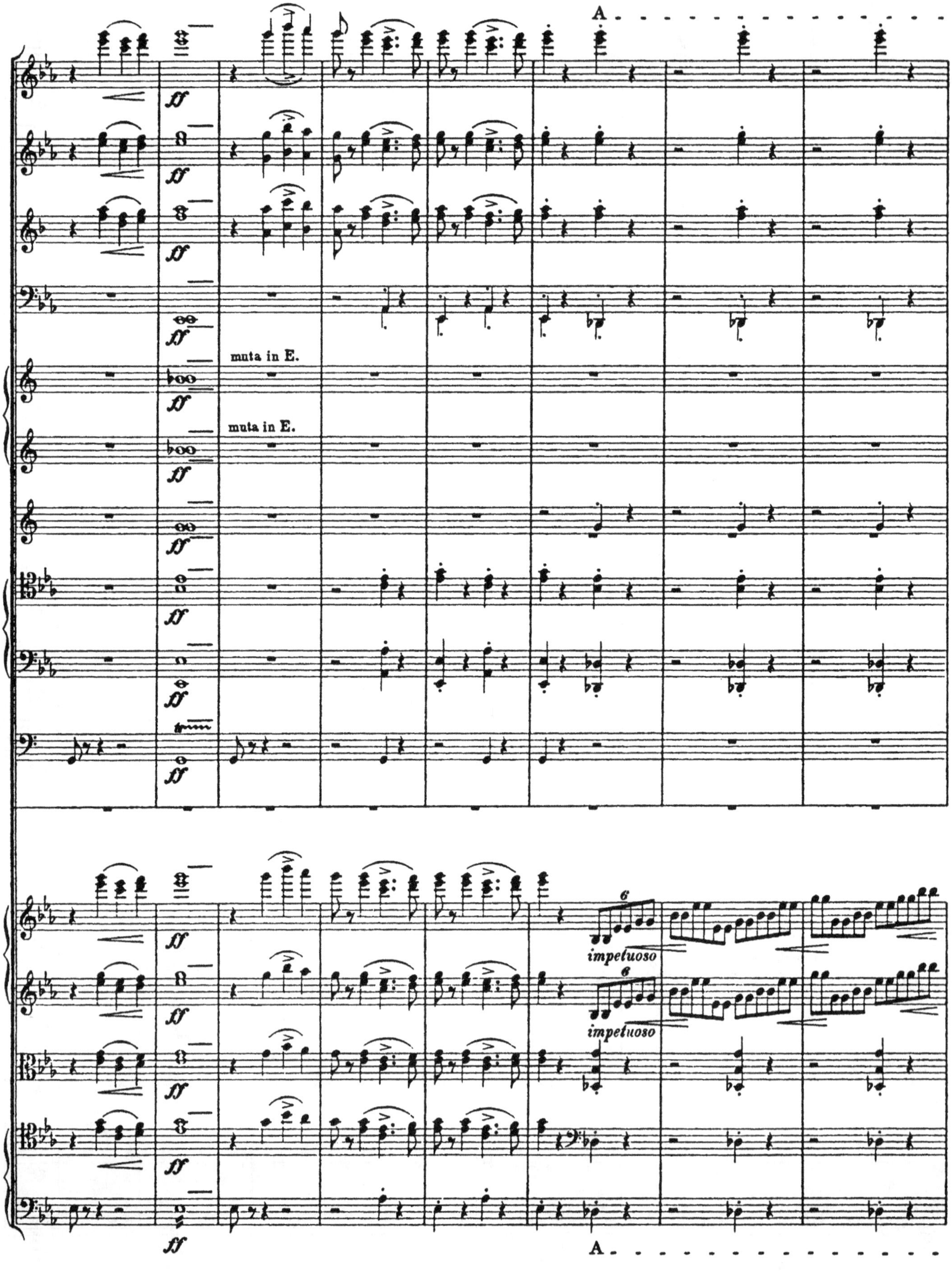
A
ff
muta in E.
muta in E.
impetuoso
6
impetuoso
6
A

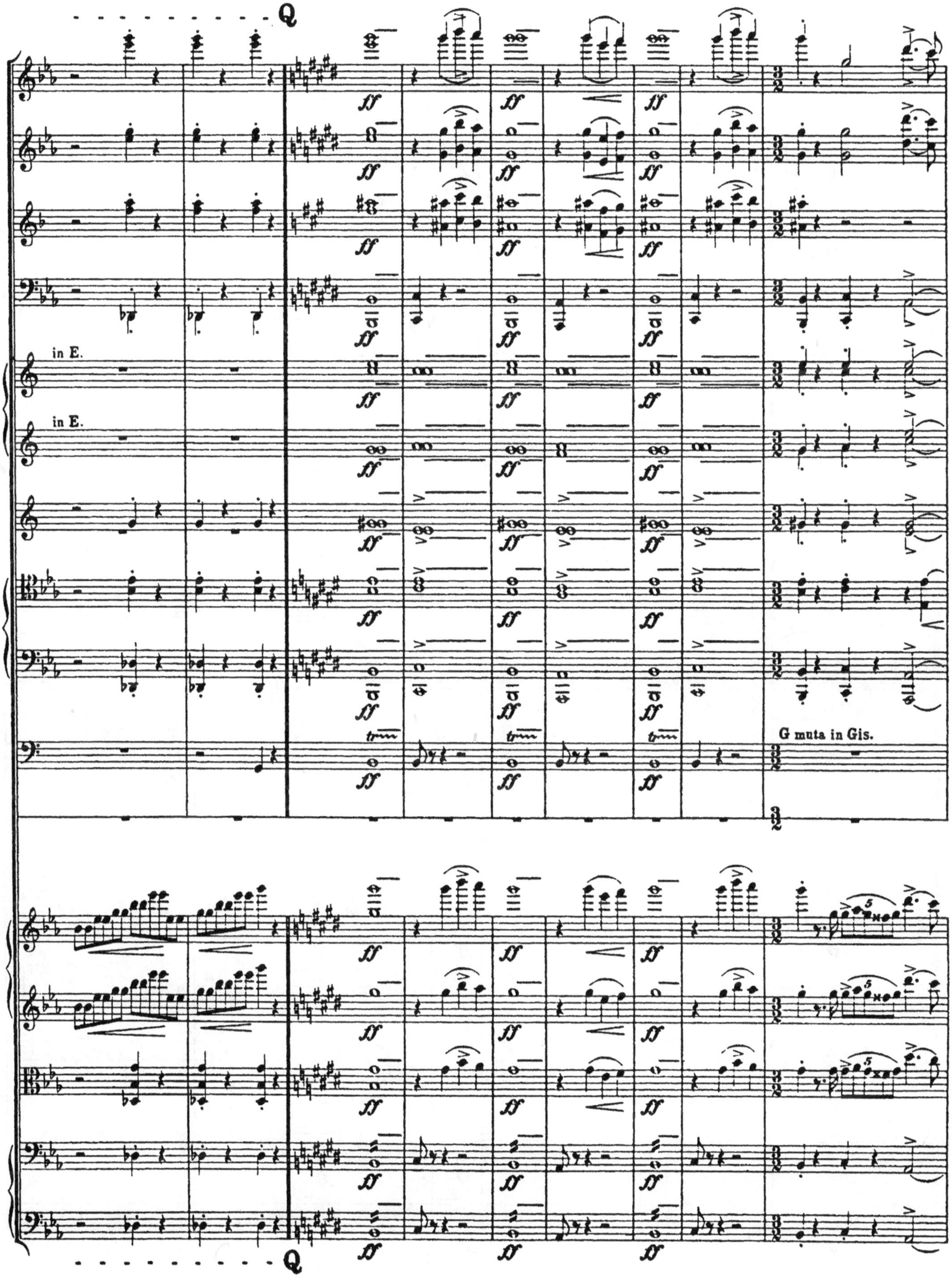
Q
in E.
in E.
G muta in Gis.
Q

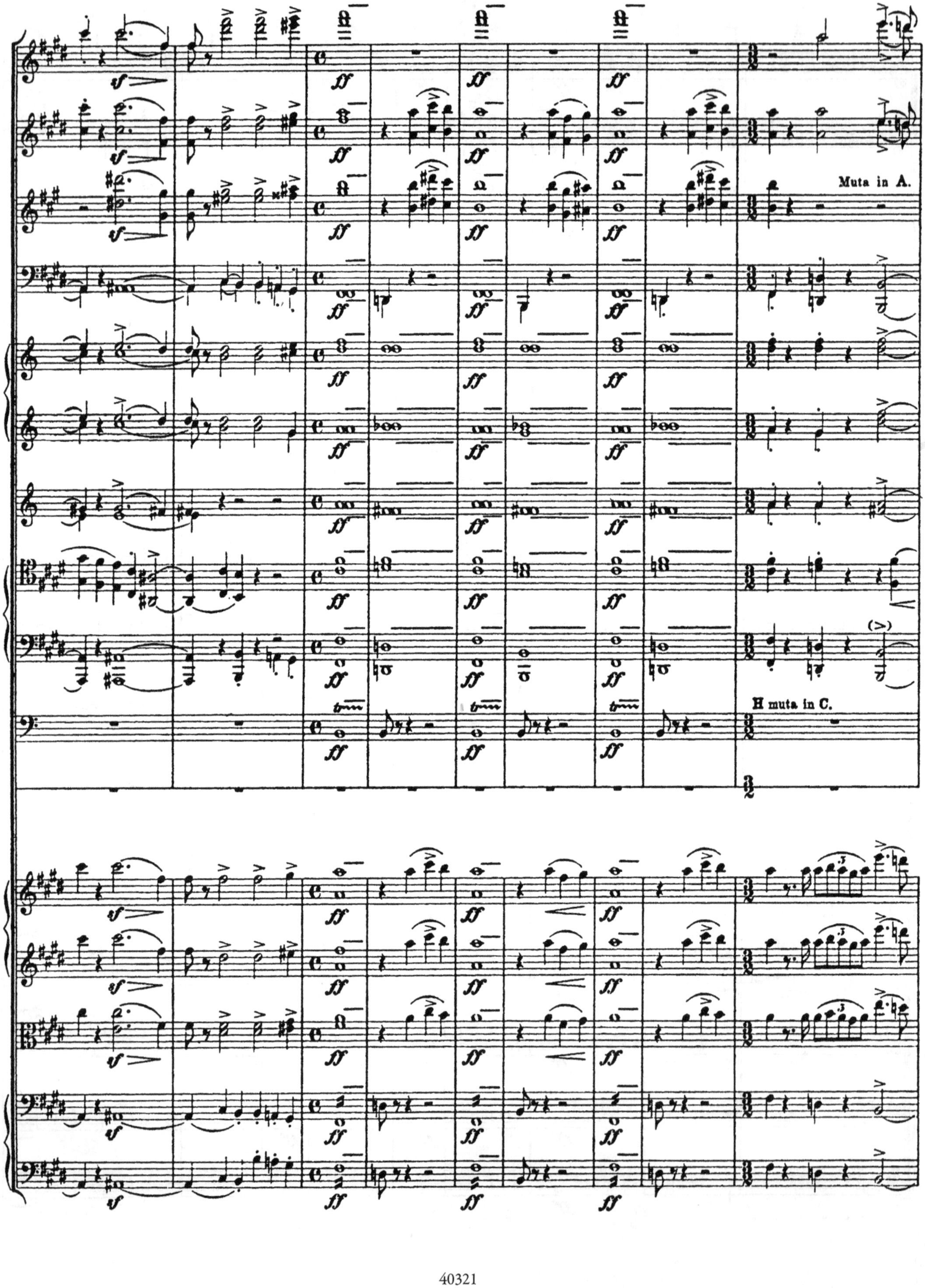
Muta in A.
H muta in C.

R
sf
dim.
>dim.
dolce espress.
dolce espress.
(in A.)
dolce espress.
dolce espress.
muta in F.
p
con grazia
(p)dolce
(p)dolce
(p)dolce
R

p
(p)
con grazia
(p)
(p)
(II. p)
con grazia
dolce espress.
dim.
con grazia
dolce espress.
(p)
dolce espress.
dolce espress.

con grazia
Solo.
dim.
p
p
(p)
(p)
dolce espress.
p
dolce espress.
p
dolce espress.
Solo.
(p)
dolce espress.

(p)
p
p
dim.
(1.p)
dim.
(p) dim.
p legato
p legato
più dimin.
perdendo
p
dim.
p
dim.
p
dim.

Enttäuschung.

Doch, ach! schon auf des Weges Mitte
Verloren die Begleiter sich;
Sie wandten treulos ihre Schritte,
Und einer nach dem andern wich.

Und immer stiller ward's und immer
Verlassner auf dem rauhen Steg.

Disillusion.

Alas! Ere past was half the distance
The company had lost their way
And concord gave way to desistence,
And, one by one, fell away

It grew more silent, dark and lonely
Each moment on the stony path.

Désenchantement.

Cette auréole hélas fut si vite voilée!
Au milieu du chemin, pleins d'infidélité,
Mes cruels compagnons de moi se détournèrent
Et disparurent tous pour ne plus revenir.

Désormais, solitude et silence planèrent
Sur le rude sentier qu'il me fallait gravir.

Andante mestoso.
a 2.
ritard.
T
dim.
pp
sf
p
p plintivo
trem.
arco
ritard.
T
Andante mestoso.

R.
p plintivo
p plintivo
p
p
pizz.
arco
espress.
p
pizz.
arco
espress.
pizz.
arco
R.

espressivo dolente
mf
sf
sf
sf
sf
espressivo dolente
mf
sf
(p) un poco marc.
8 Bässe. pizz.
divisi (p)

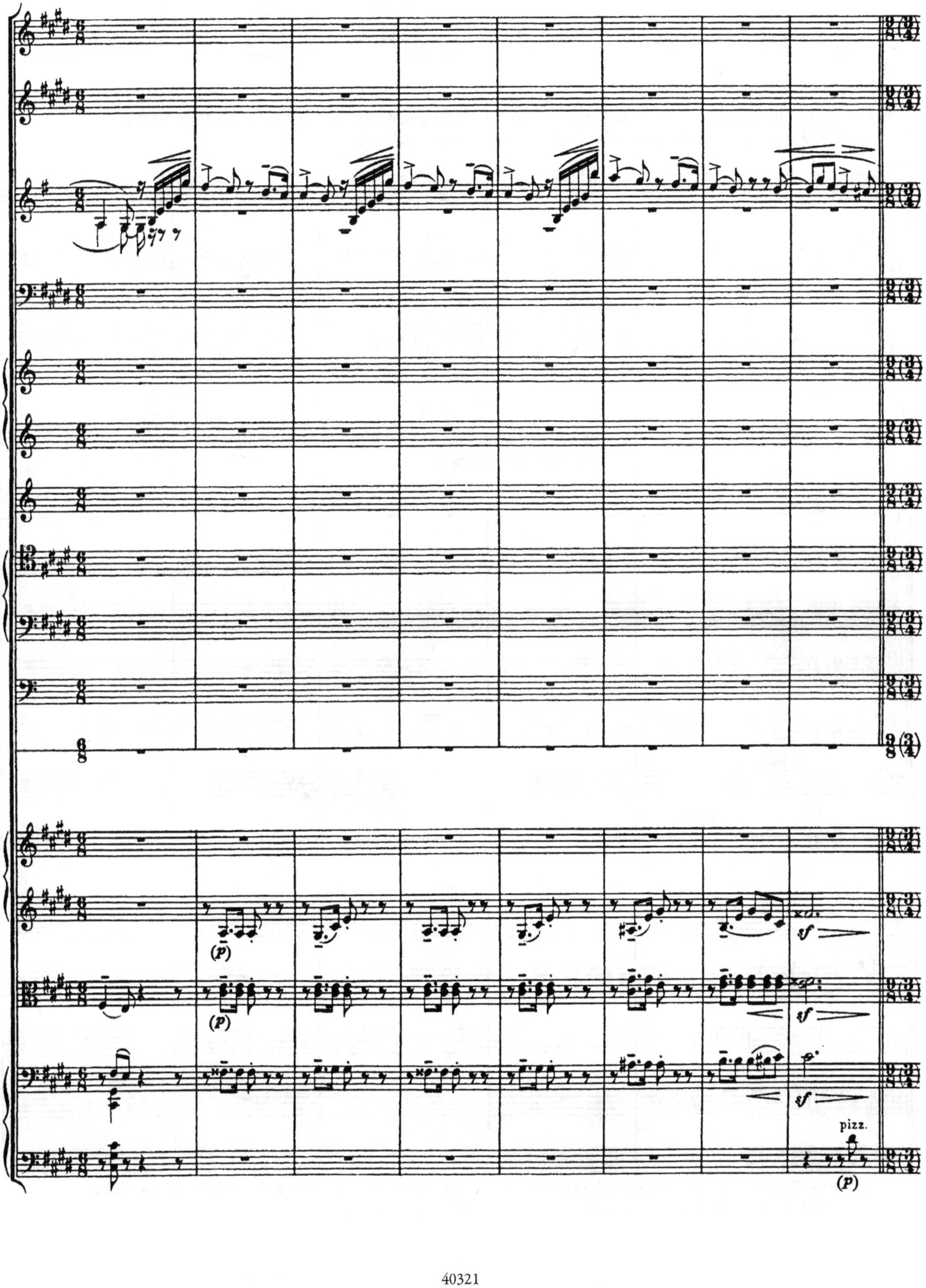
(p)
(p)
sf
sf
sf
pizz.
(p)

Von all dem rauschenden Geleite	Of all who with me gaily started	Après avoir perdu mon escorte enivrante
Wer harrte liebend bei mir aus?	Did one in pity by me stay?	Qui reste près de moi pour calmer mon tourment,
Wer steht mir tröstend noch zur Seite	Who had not coldly from me parted,	Pour tâcher de guérir ma blessure saignante,
Und folgt mir bis zum finstern Haus?	Abandoned me upon my way?	Pour soutenir mes pas à mon dernier moment?

U Das Tempo allmählich etwas bewegter bis zu dem Buchstaben **W** und drei Schläge im Takt.
Poco a poco più animato sin alla lettera W battendo ¾.

U Das Tempo allmählich etwas bewegter bis zu dem Buchstaben **W** und drei Schläge im Takt.
Poco a poco più animato sin alla lettera W battendo ¾.

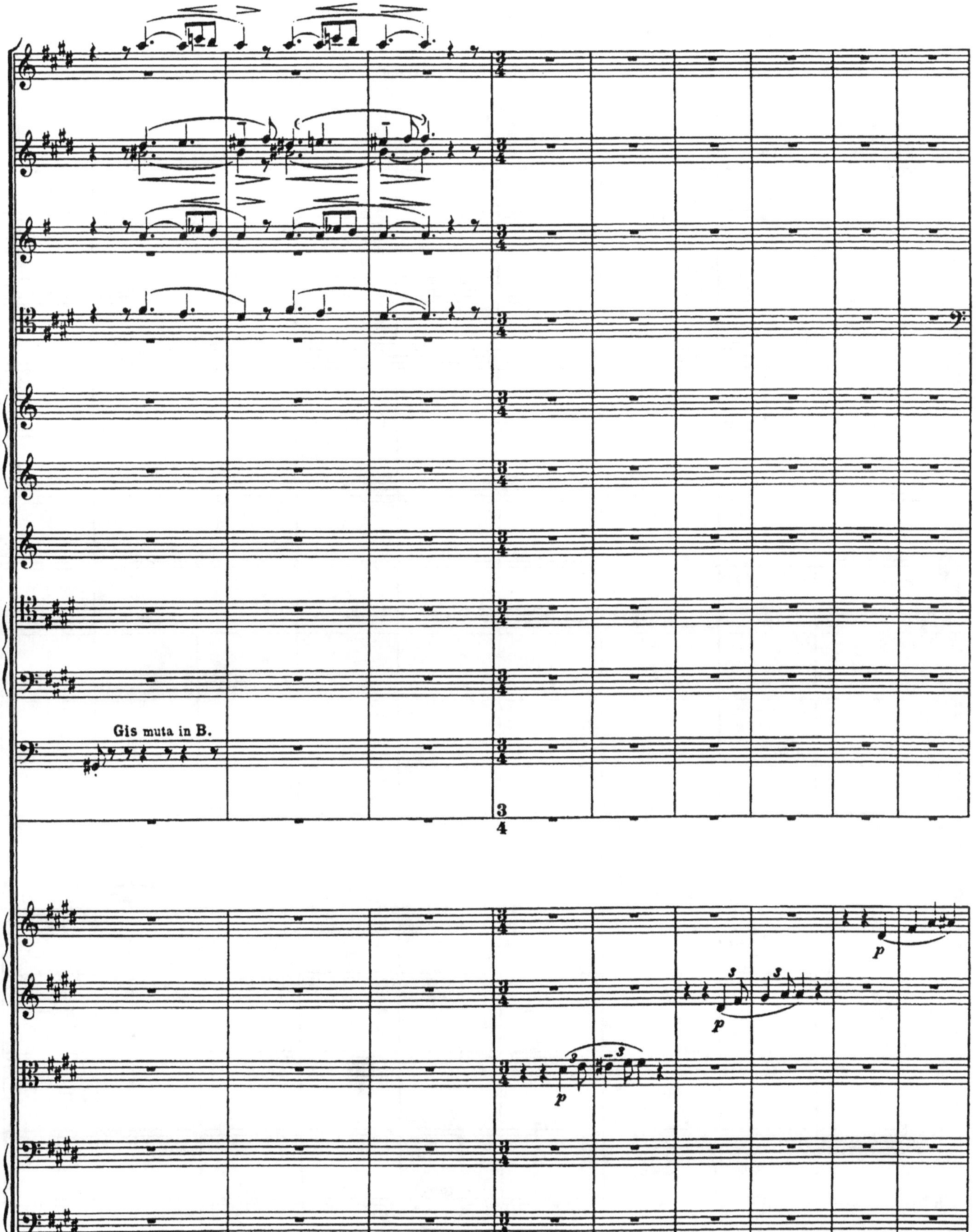
Gis muta in B.
p
p
p

Du, die du alle Wunden heilest,
Der Freundschaft leise, zarte Hand,
Des Lebens Bürden liebend teilest,
Du, die ich frühe sucht' und fand!

Yea, one! For others' wounds thou carest.
True Friendship, with thy tender hand
Thou others' sorrows gladly sharest—
Thy love through all doth steadfast stand.

C'est toi, noble amitié, que j'ai bientôt trouvée,
Toi qui panses le cœur de ta légère main,
Toujours présente à l'heure où l'âme est éprouvée,
Adoucissant toujours notre sombre destin.

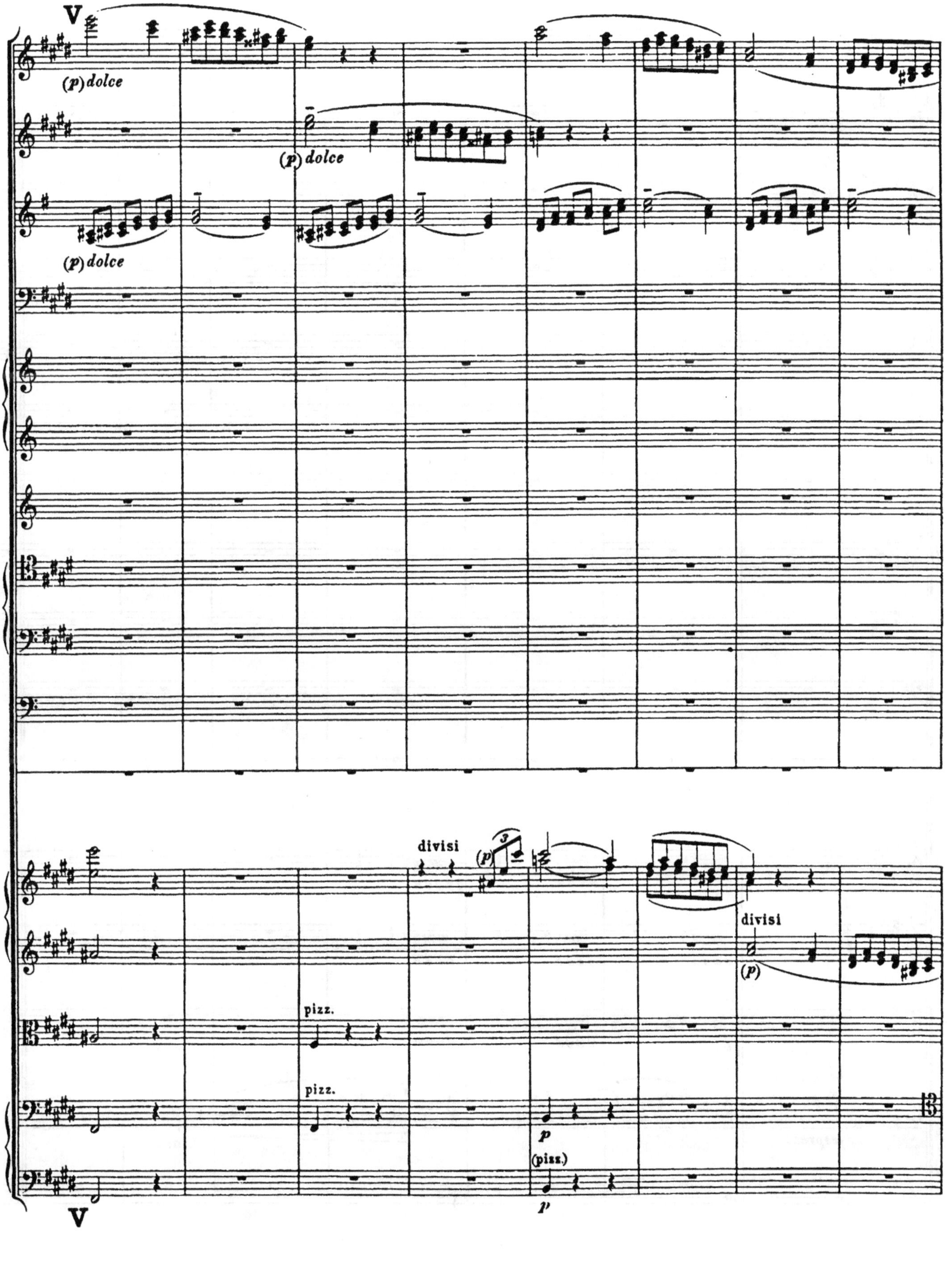
V
(p) dolce
(p) dolce
(p) dolce
divisi
(p)
3
divisi
(p)
pizz.
pizz.
p
(pizz.)
p
V

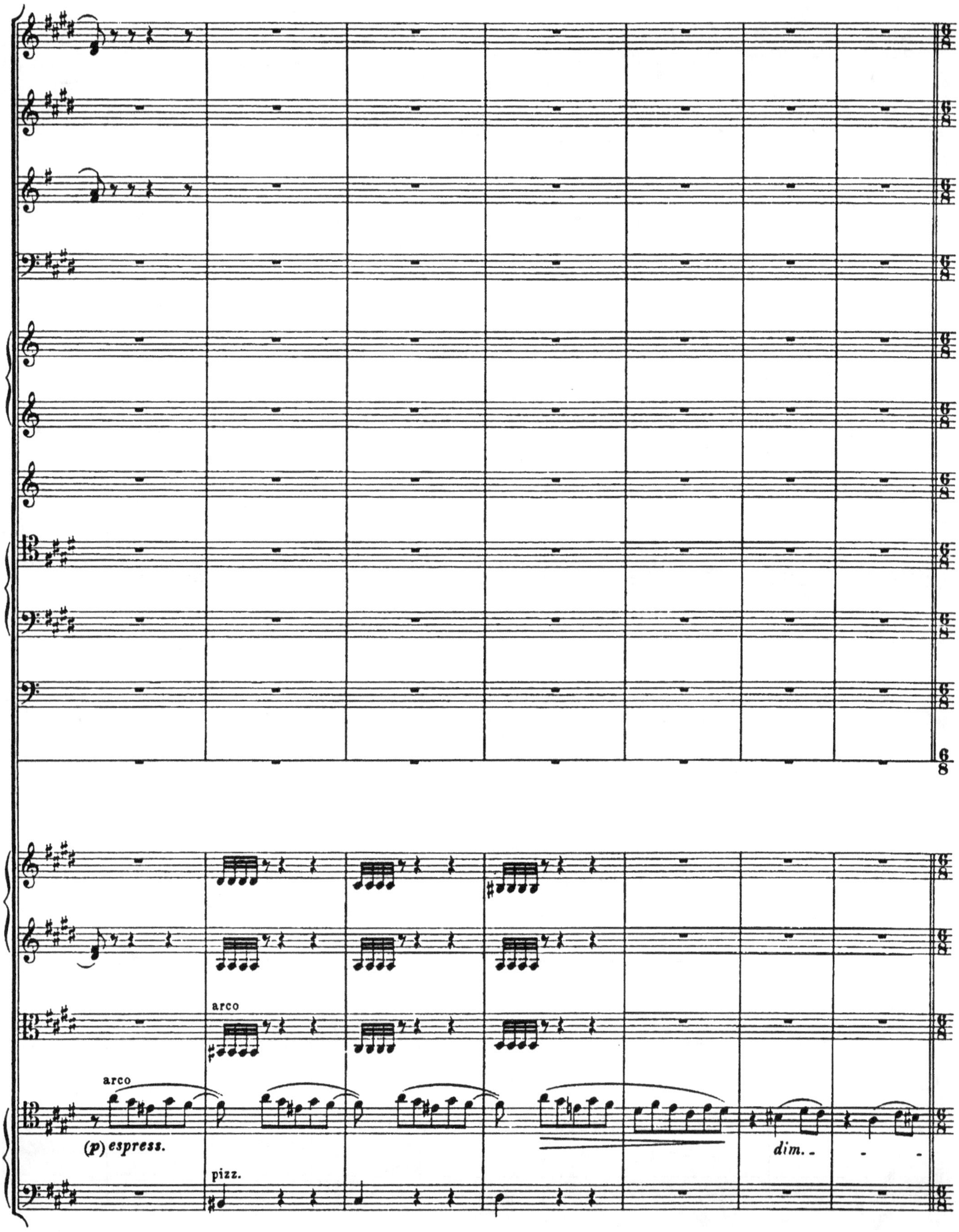
arco
pizz.
arco
(p) espress.
dim.

W Andante mestoso.

(p)

(p)

in E.

(p) espress. dolente

sf

6/8 **9/8** **6/8**

(p)

pizz.

(p)

pizz.

Violoncell-Solo.

(p)

(p) espress. dolente

sf

Die übrigen Vcelle u. Kbässe.
The other Celli and Basses.
Les autres Vcelles et Basses.

pizz.

p

W Andante mestoso.

(p)espress. dolente
(p)espress. dolente
a 2.
p
sf
p
arco
arco
(arco) Tutti.
(p)
sf

Vom Buchstaben X an zwei Schläge im Takt.
Dalla lettera X si batte 2/4.
X
p
plintiro
a 2.
muta in E.
sf
sf
sf
X
Vom Buchstaben X an zwei Schläge im Takt.
Dalla lettera X si batte 2/4.

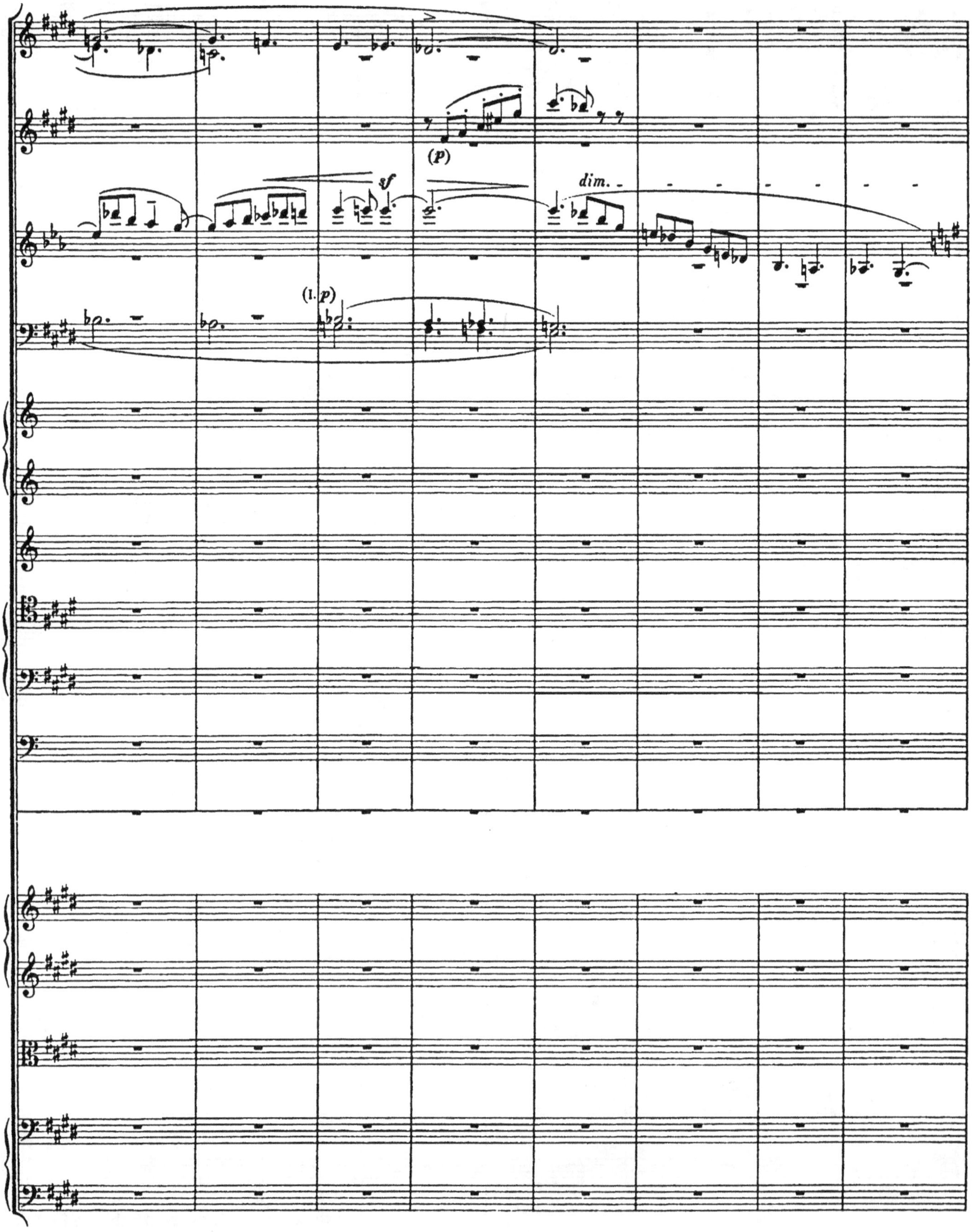
(p)
sf
dim.
(1. p)

Beschäftigung.

Und du, die gern sich mit ihr gattet,
Wie sie der Seele Sturm beschwört,
Beschäftigung, die nie ermattet,
Die langsam schafft, doch nie zerstört,
Die zu dem Bau der Ewigkeiten
Zwar Sandkorn nur für Sandkorn reicht,
Doch von der grossen Schuld der Zeiten
Minuten, Tage, Jahre streicht.—

Employment.

And thou, who'rt with her long since married,
The soul's storm, too, thou quickly curbst
Employment, ne'er thy work miscarried—
Though slow thou buildst, thou ne'er disturbst.
Thy toil Eternity engages.
Thereto it atom-like appears,
Yet from the mighty debt of ages
It strikes off minutes, days and years.

Travail.

Et toi, calmant-aussi les orages de l'âme,
Toi qu'avec l'amitié dans mon cœur j'unissais,
Toi qui brûles toujours d'une puissante flamme,
Qui produis lentement, mais ne détruis jamais,
Saint amour du travail qui n'apportes sans doute
Que quelques grains de sable au grand œuvre éternel,
Mais qui, sans te lasser, du temps la longue route
Effaces, délivrant l'infortuné mortel.

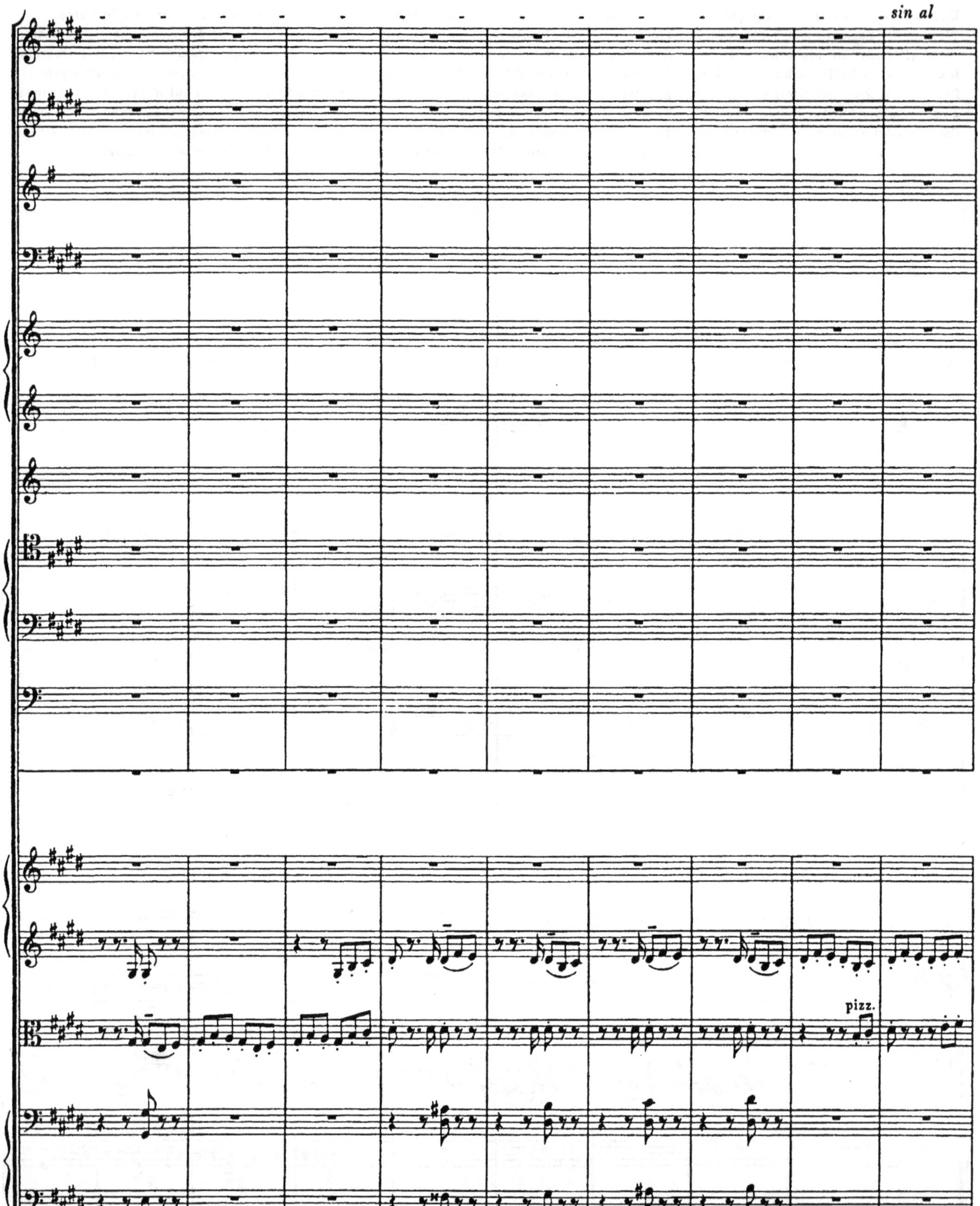
sin al
pizz.
sin al

Y Allegretto mosso.

Y Allegretto mosso.

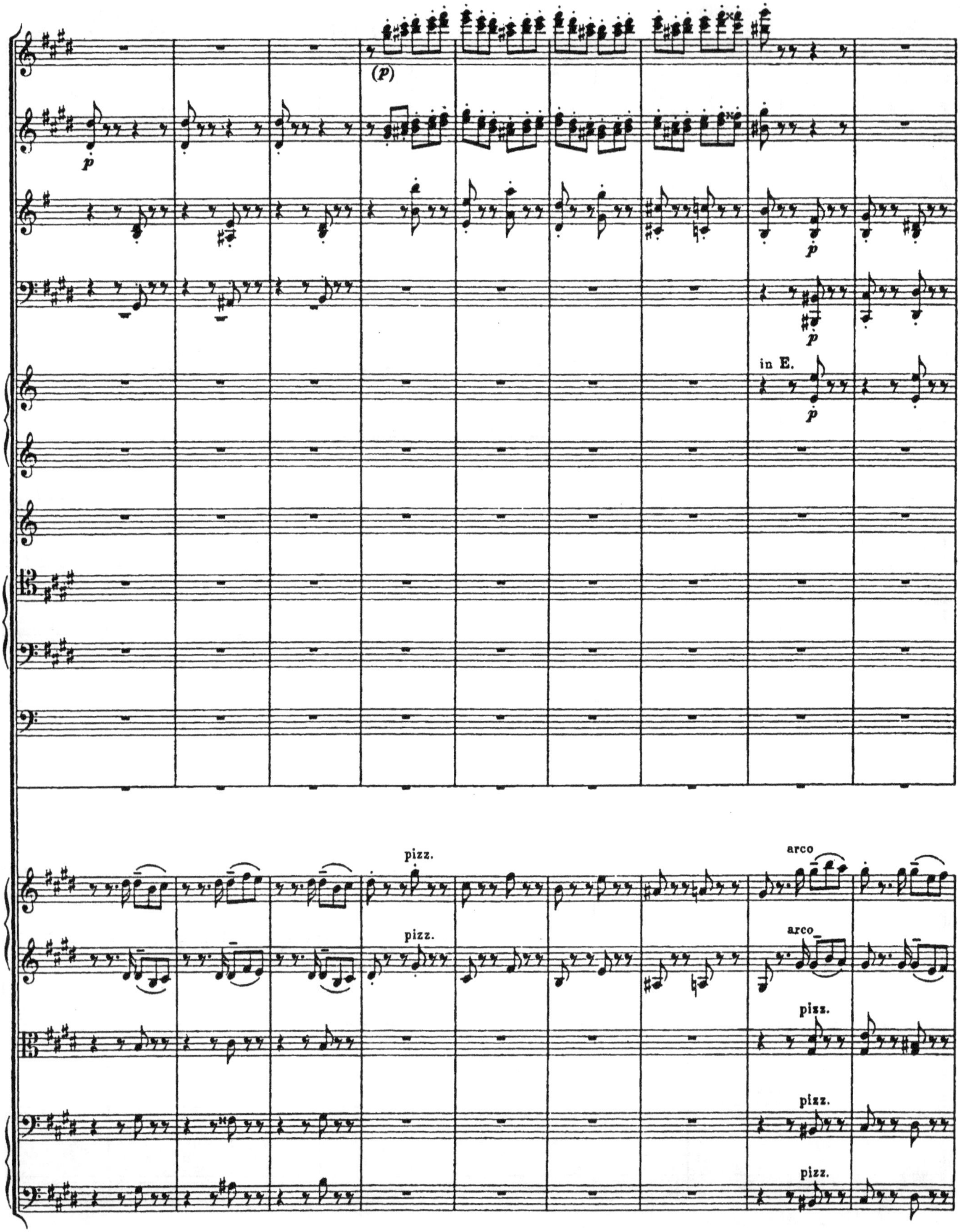
(p)
p
in E.
pizz.
arco

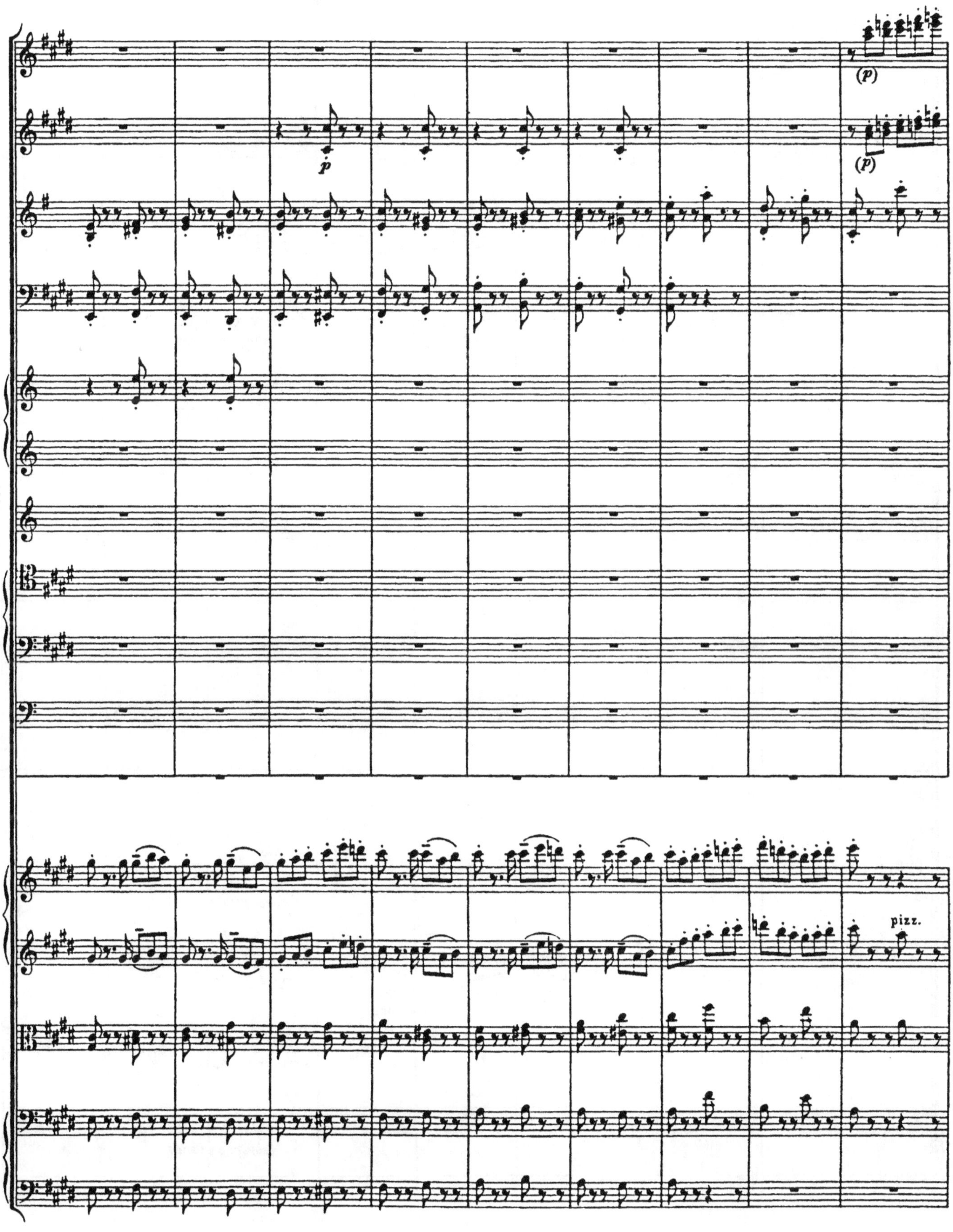
(p)
p
(p)
pizz.

Z
sempre piano
sempre piano
pizz.
arco
sempre piano
arco
sempre piano
pizz.
sempre piano
pizz.
(sempre piano)
Z

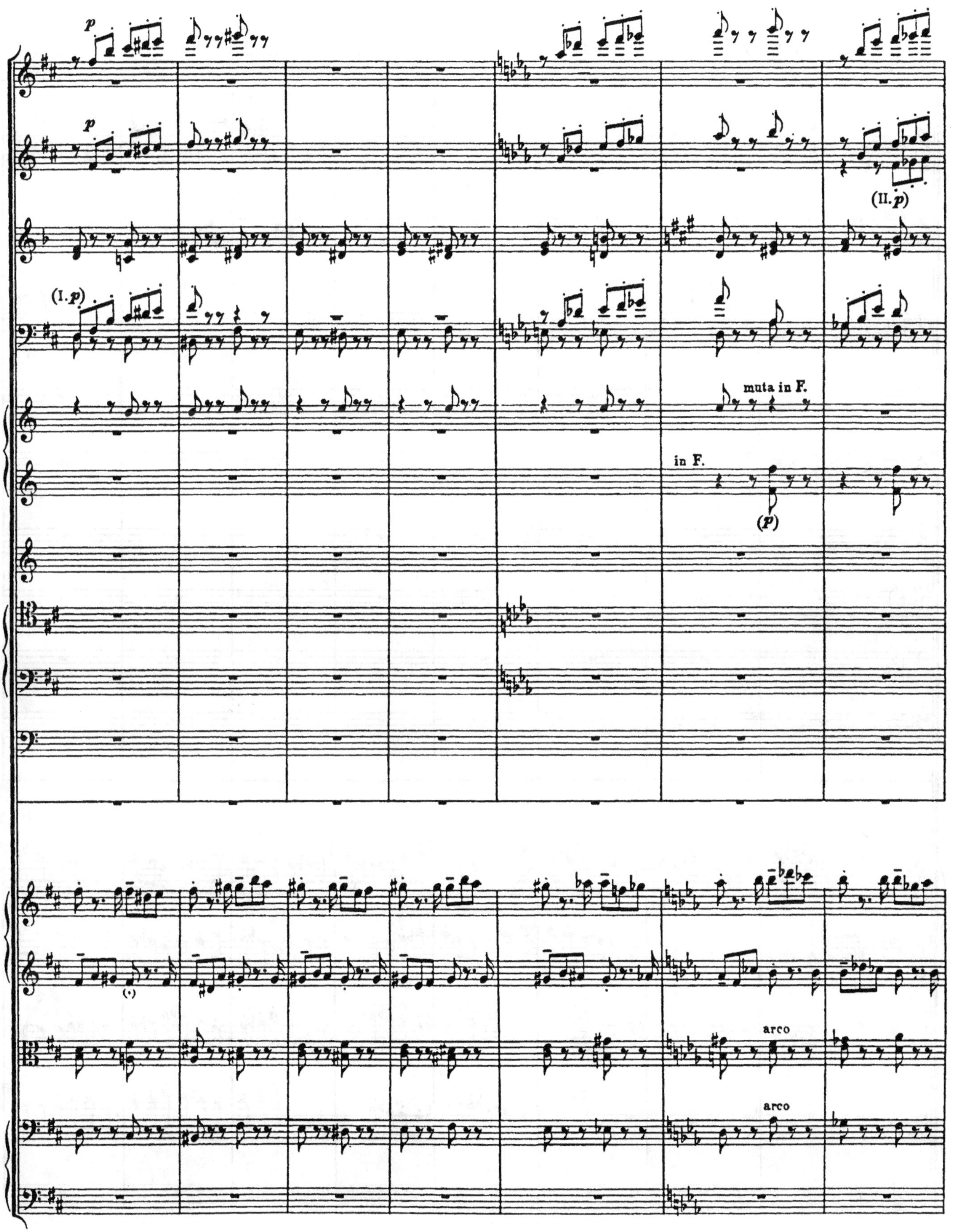

p
p
(II. p)
(I. p)
muta in F.
in F.
(p)
arco
arco

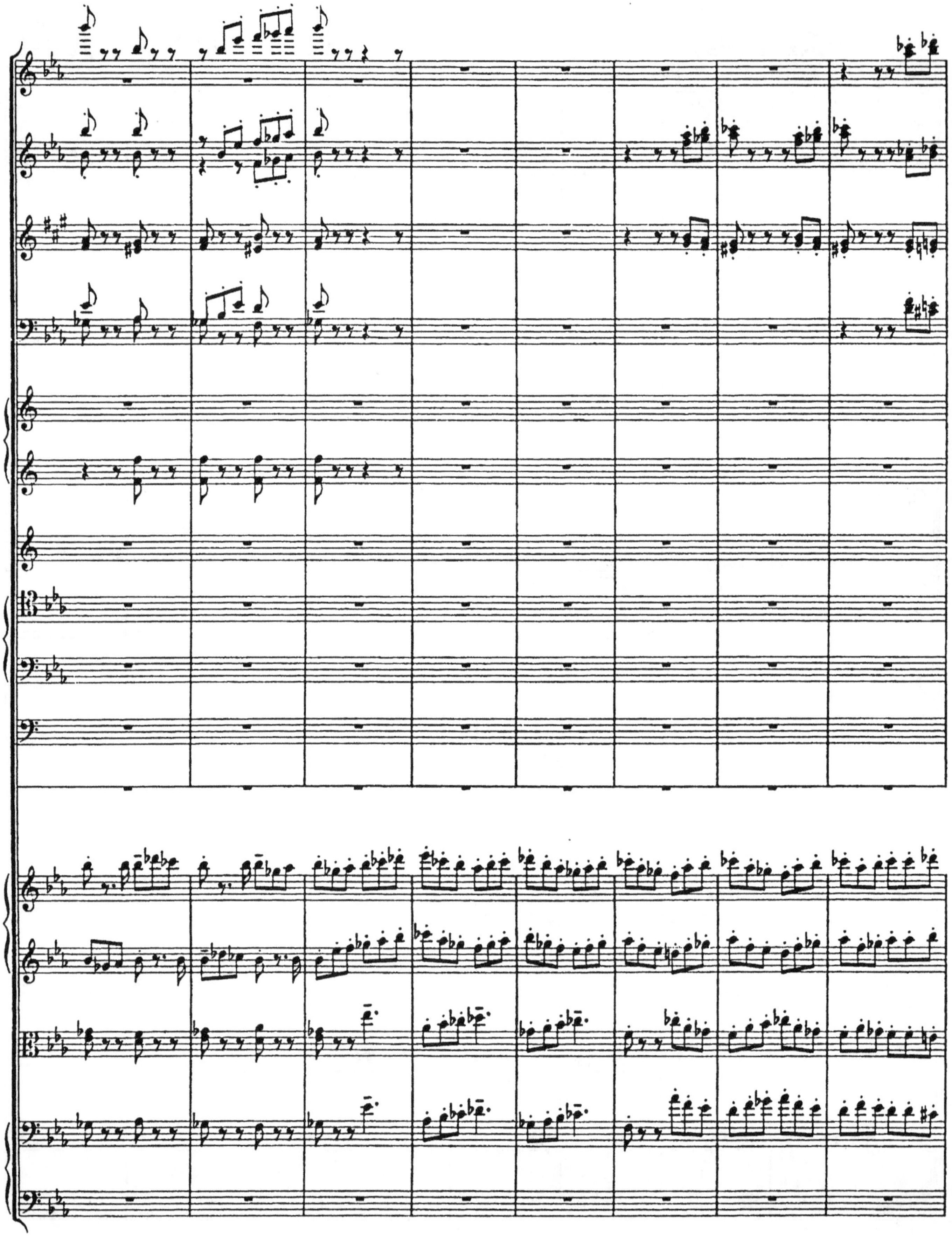

Tz
p
a 2.
p
a 2.
p
p
p
p
p
p
p
p
p
p
arco
sempre p e stacc.
sempre p e stacc.
Tz

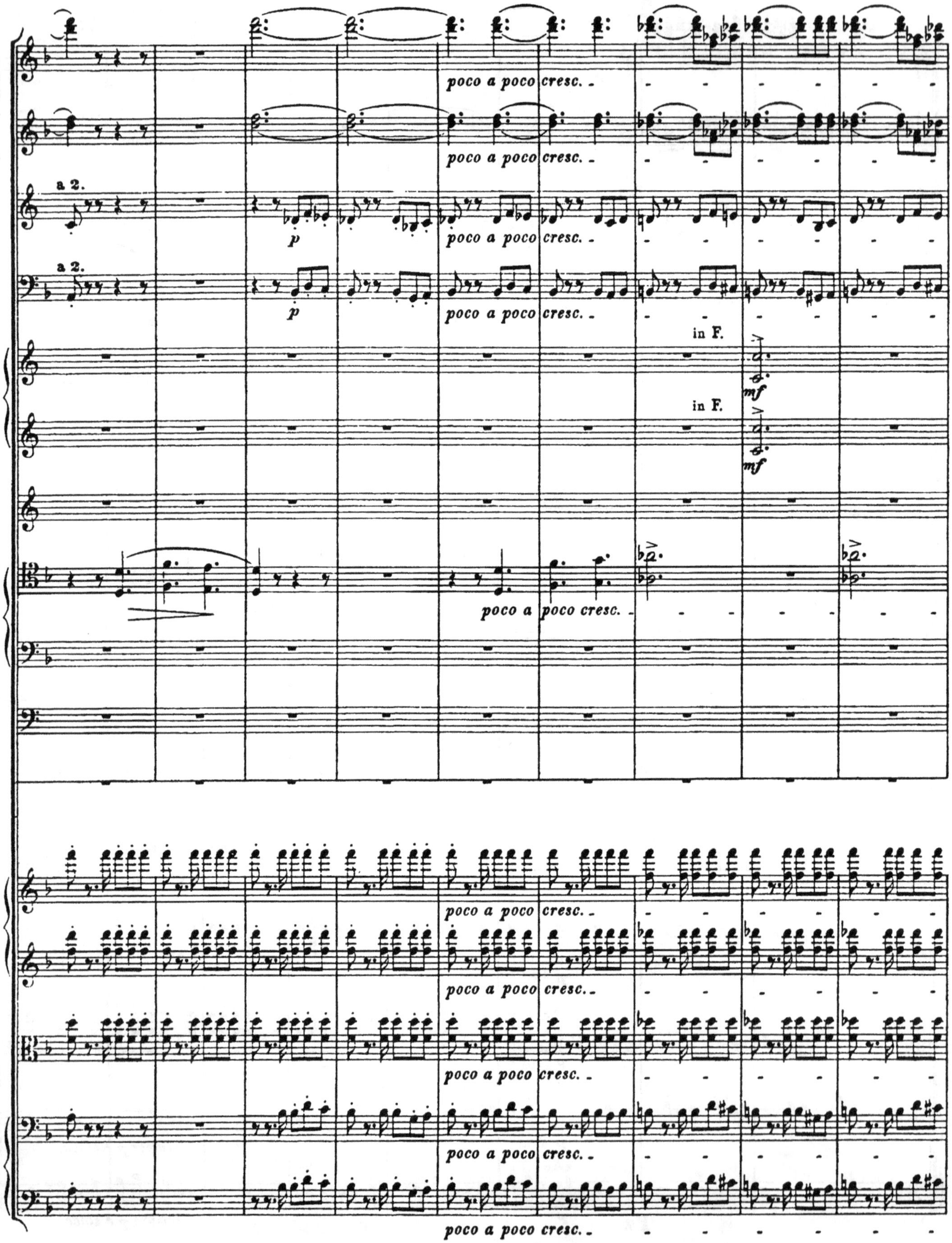
a 2.
a 2.
p
p
poco a poco cresc.
in F.
in F.
mf
mf
poco a poco cresc.

Allegro spiritoso molto.

muta in B.

rinforz.

rinforz.

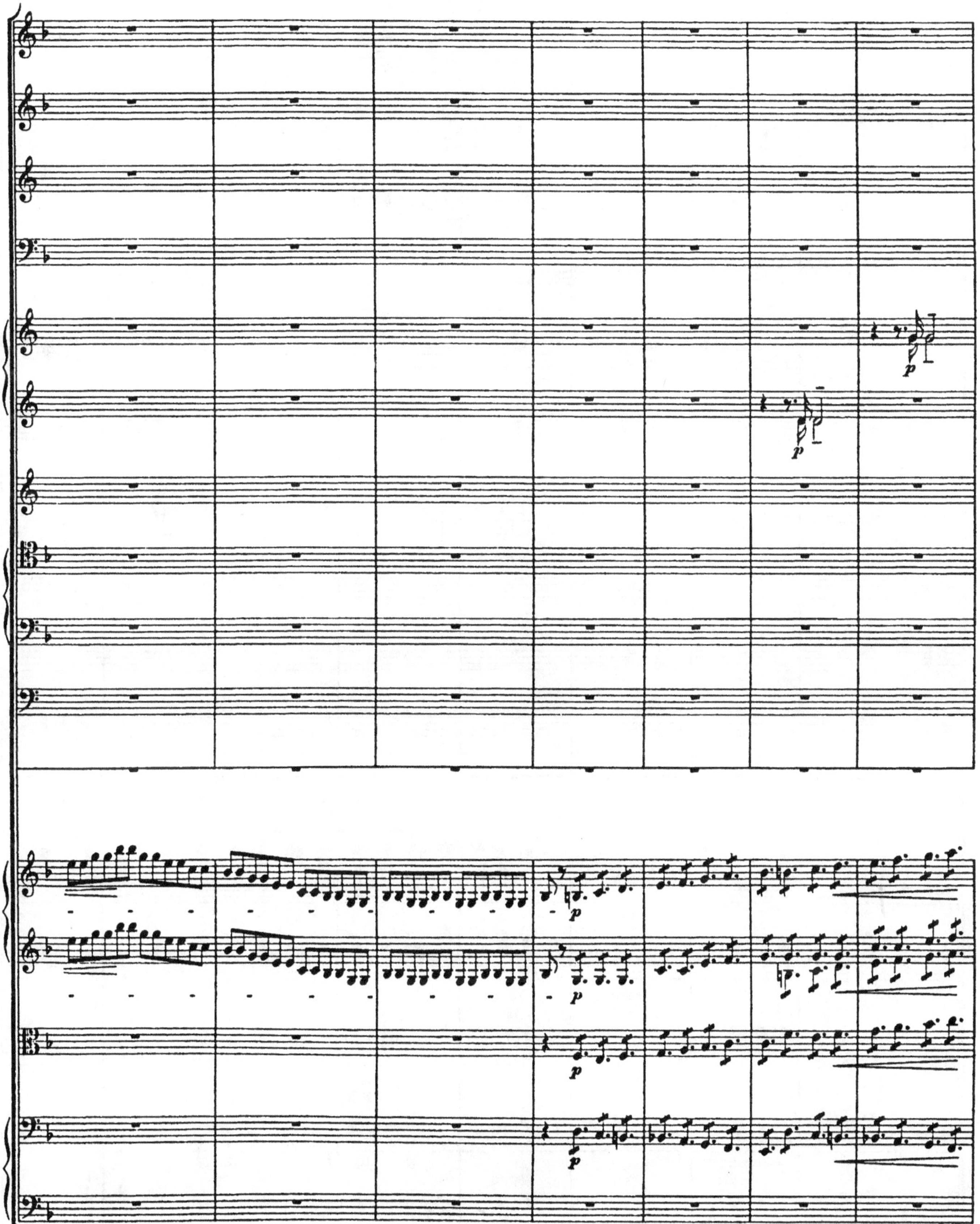
p
p
p
p
p
p
p

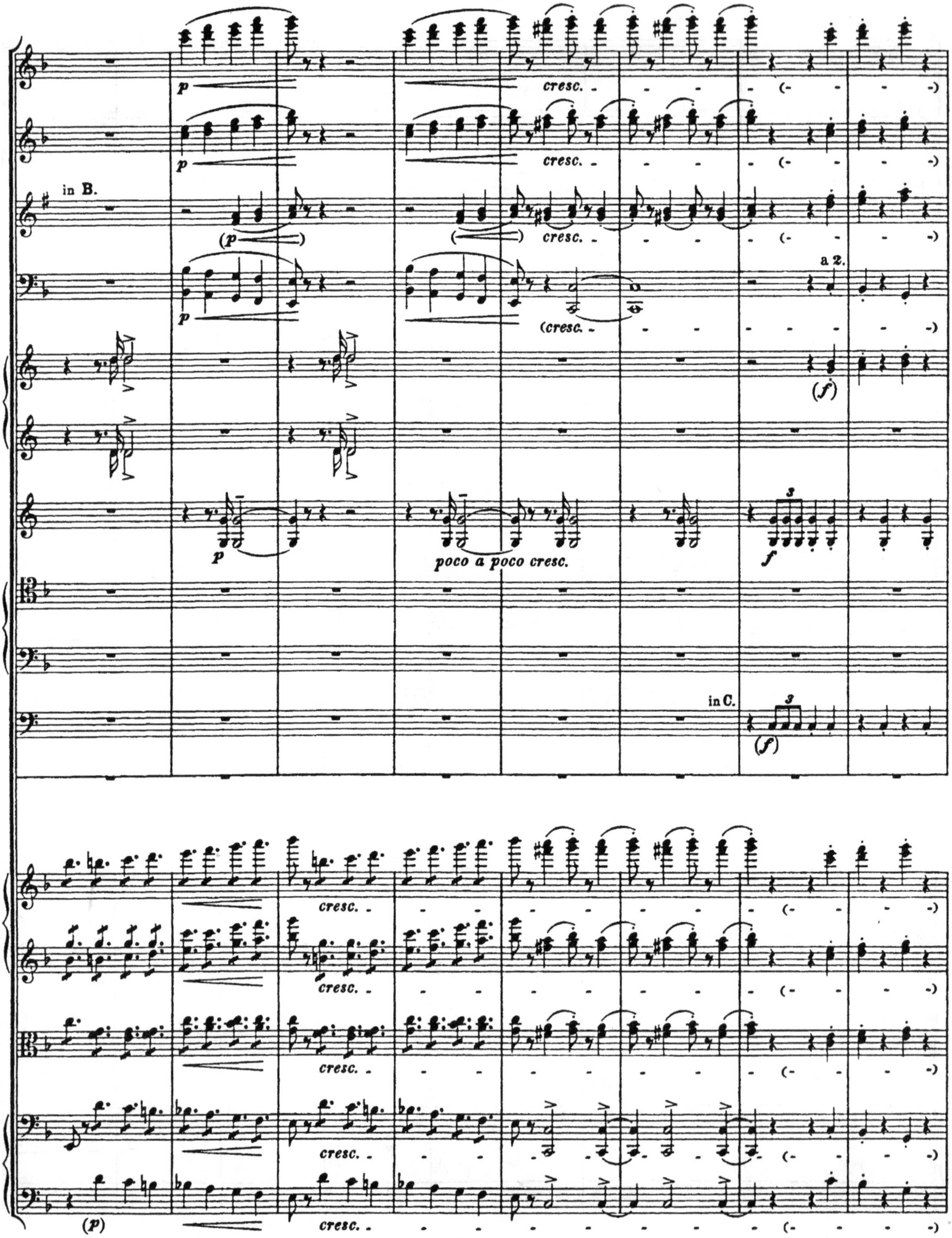
in B.
a 2.
in C.
p
cresc.
(p
(cresc.
(f)
poco a poco cresc.
f
(p)

Apotheose.*)

Più moderato, maestoso, con somma passione.

Bb Più moderato, maestoso, con somma passione.

*) Das Festhalten und dabei die unaufhaltsame Betätigung des Ideals ist unsers Lebens höchster Zweck. In diesem Sinne erlaubte ich mir das Schiller'sche Gedicht zu ergänzen durch die jubelnd bekräftigende Wiederaufnahme der im ersten Satz vorausgegangenen Motive als Schluss-Apotheose.

The firm adhesion to and therewith the ceaseless cooperation of the Ideal is the highest aim of life on earth. It was in this sense that I took the liberty to supplement Schiller's poem by adding as closing apotheosis the jubilant confirmatory resumption of the motive which had gone before in the first part.

La foi en l'idéal, à la réalisation duquel nous ne pouvons pas nous empêcher de participer, est le but suprême de notre vie. C'est dans ce sens que reprenant les motifs contenus déjà dans la première partie je me suis permis de compléter et confirmer la poésie de Schiller par une apothéose finale retentissante d'allégresse.

F. Liszt.

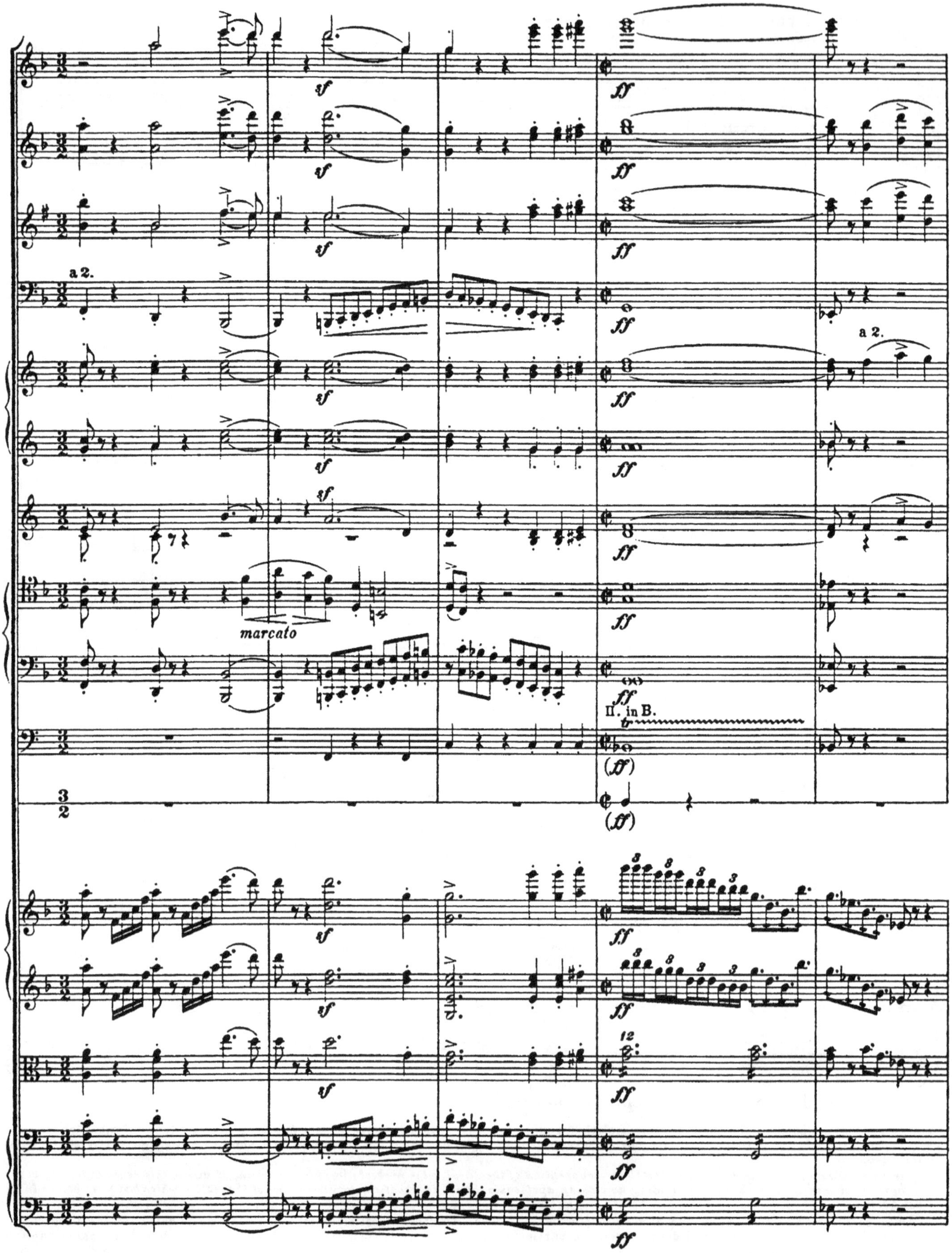
a 2.
a 2.
marcato
II. in B.
sf
ff
(ff)

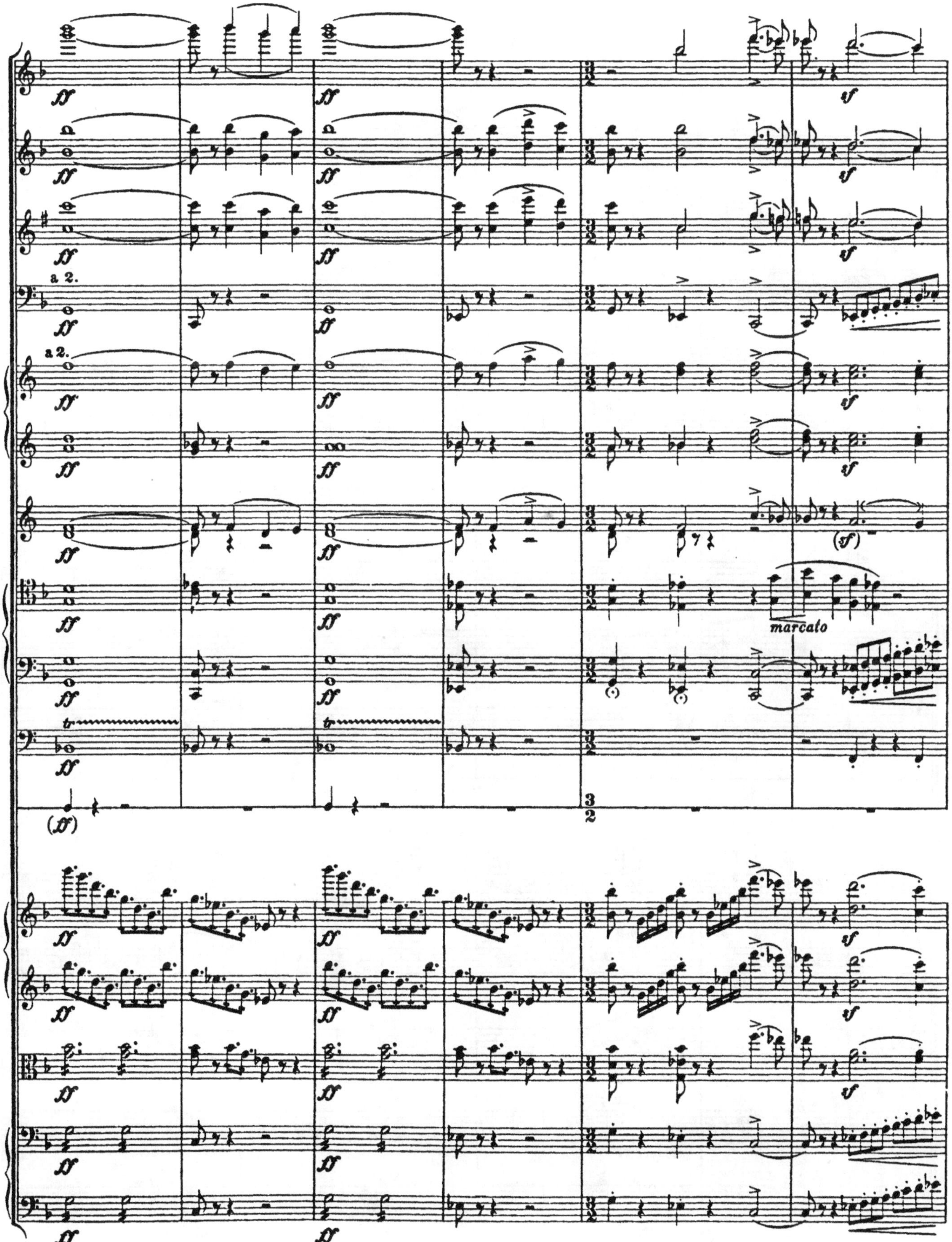
a 2.
a 2.
marcato

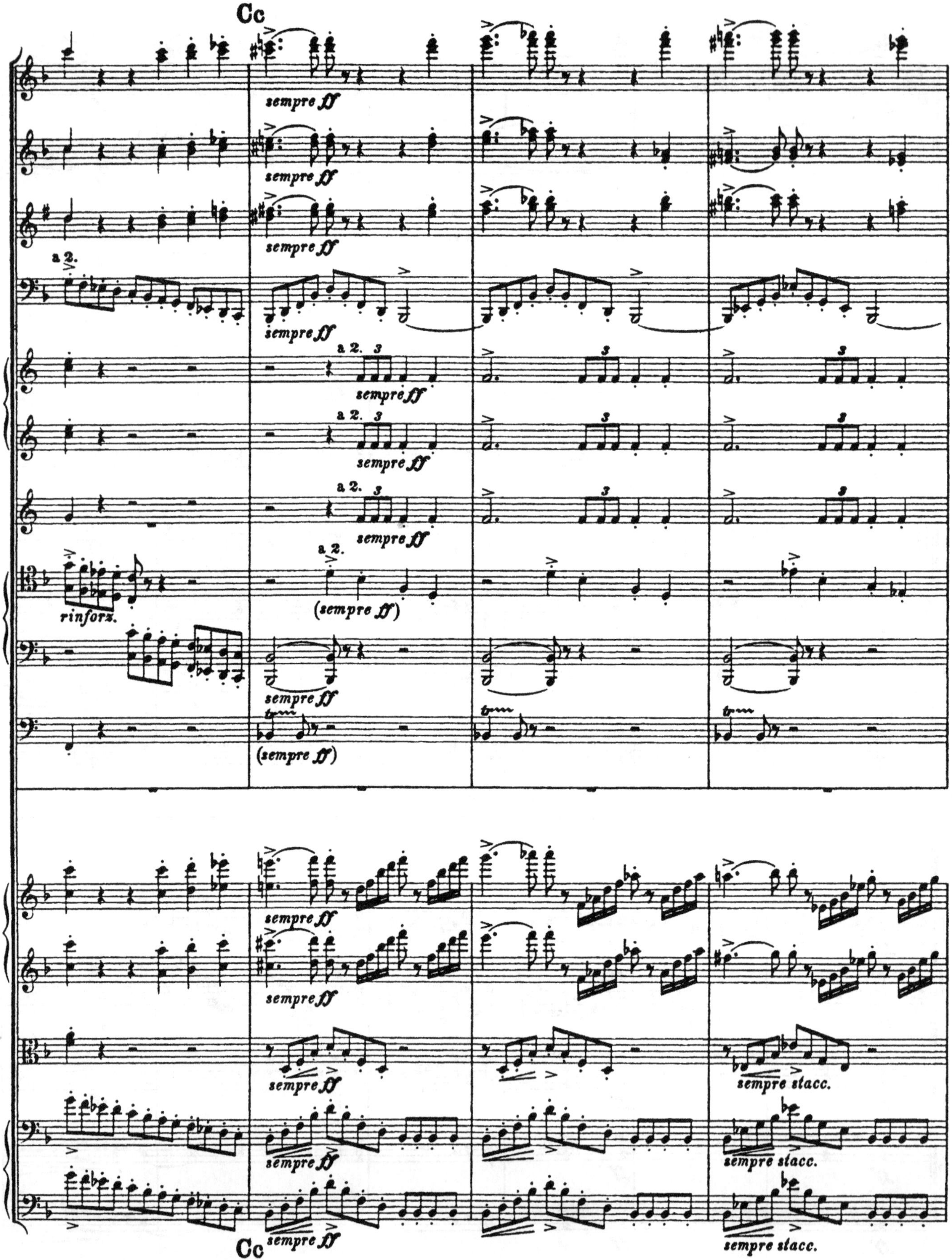
Cc
sempre ff
a 2.
rinforz.
(sempre ff)
sempre stacc.
Cc

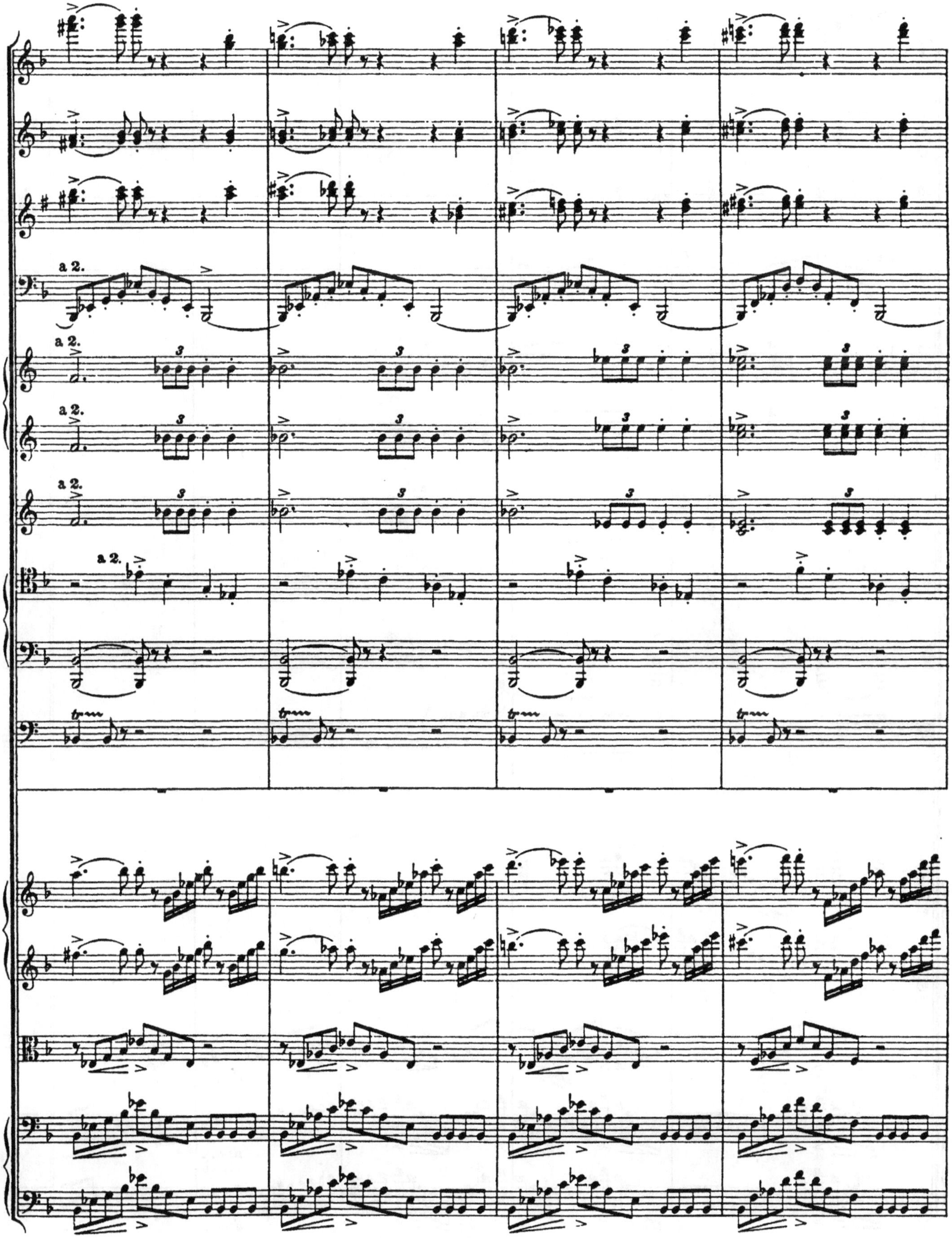
a 2.
a 2.
a 2.
a 2.
a 2.

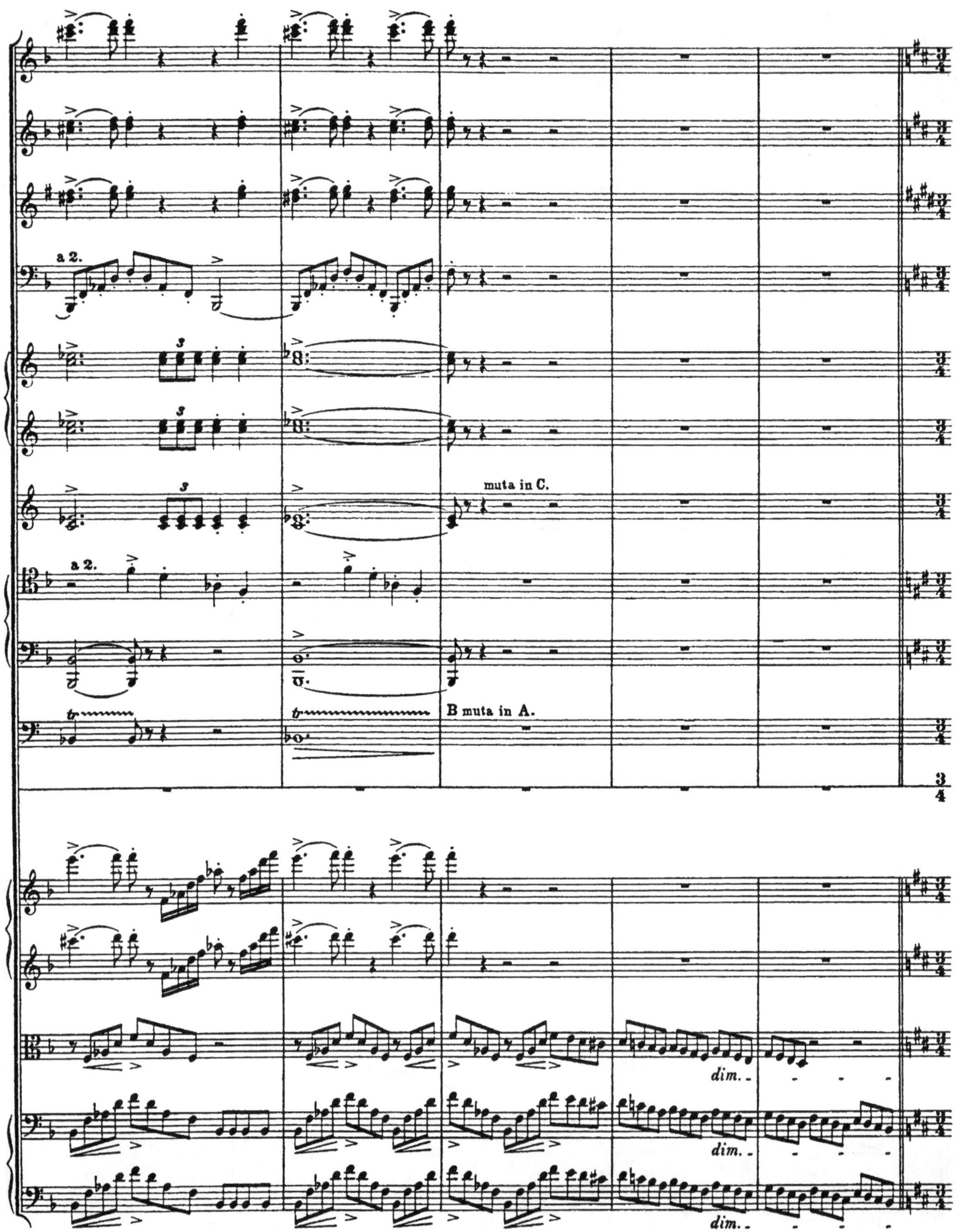
a 2.
muta in C.
a 2.
B muta in A.
dim.

Allegro vivace.
Dd
p leggiero
p leggiero
p leggiero
p leggiero
p
p leggiero
p sempre stacc.
p leggiero
p sempre stacc.
p leggiero
p sempre stacc.
trillo
p
(p)
pizz.
Dd Allegro vivace.

p leggiero
p
p leggiero
p leggiero
p
p leggiero
p
p leggiero
p leggiero
p leggiero
p stacc.
arco
p stacc.
p
pizz.

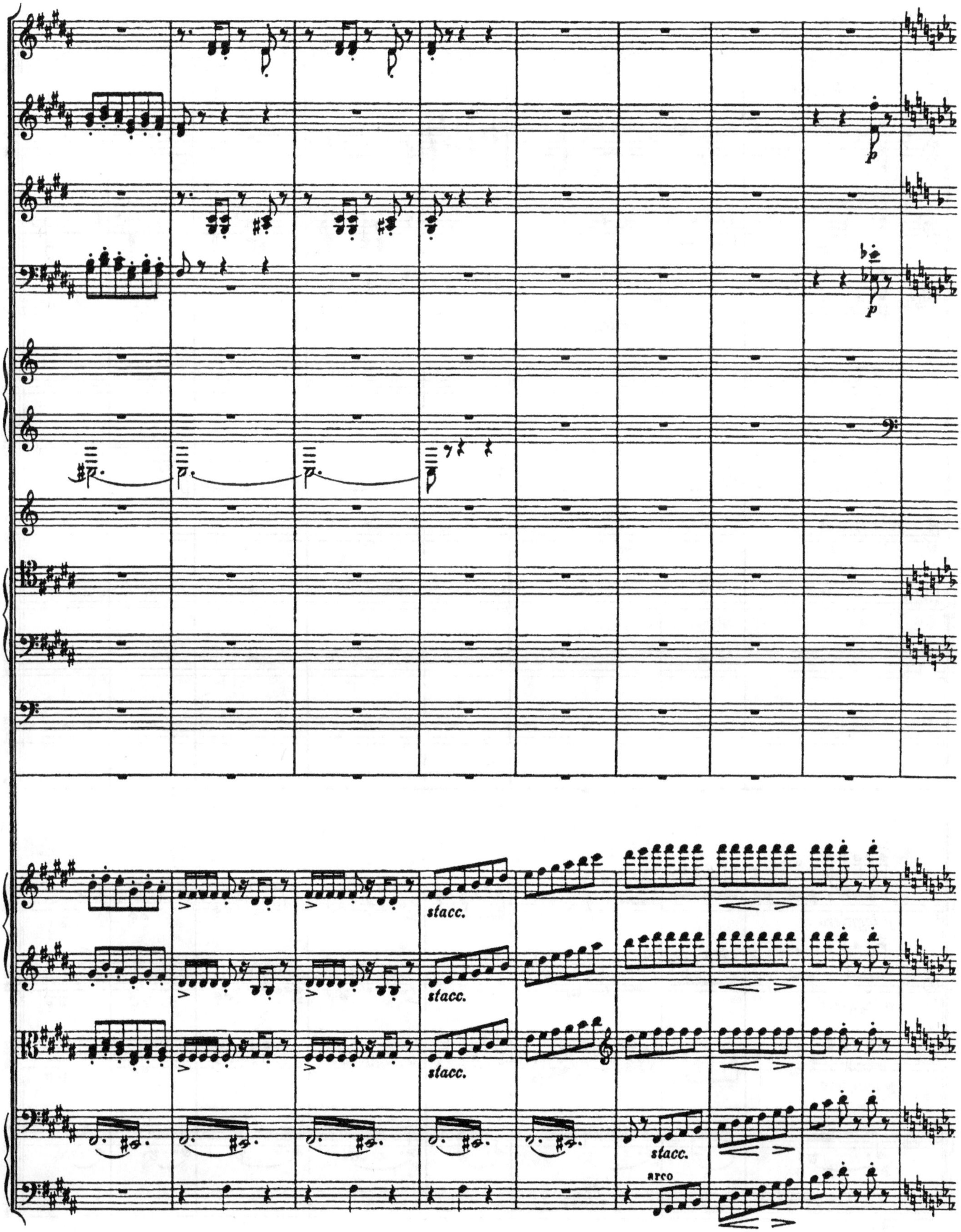
p
p
stacc.
stacc.
stacc.
stacc.
arco

Ee
p leggiero
p leggiero
p leggiero
p leggiero
p
p leggiero
p leggiero
p leggiero
p
pizz.
(p)
Ee

Allegro vivace (ma non troppo).

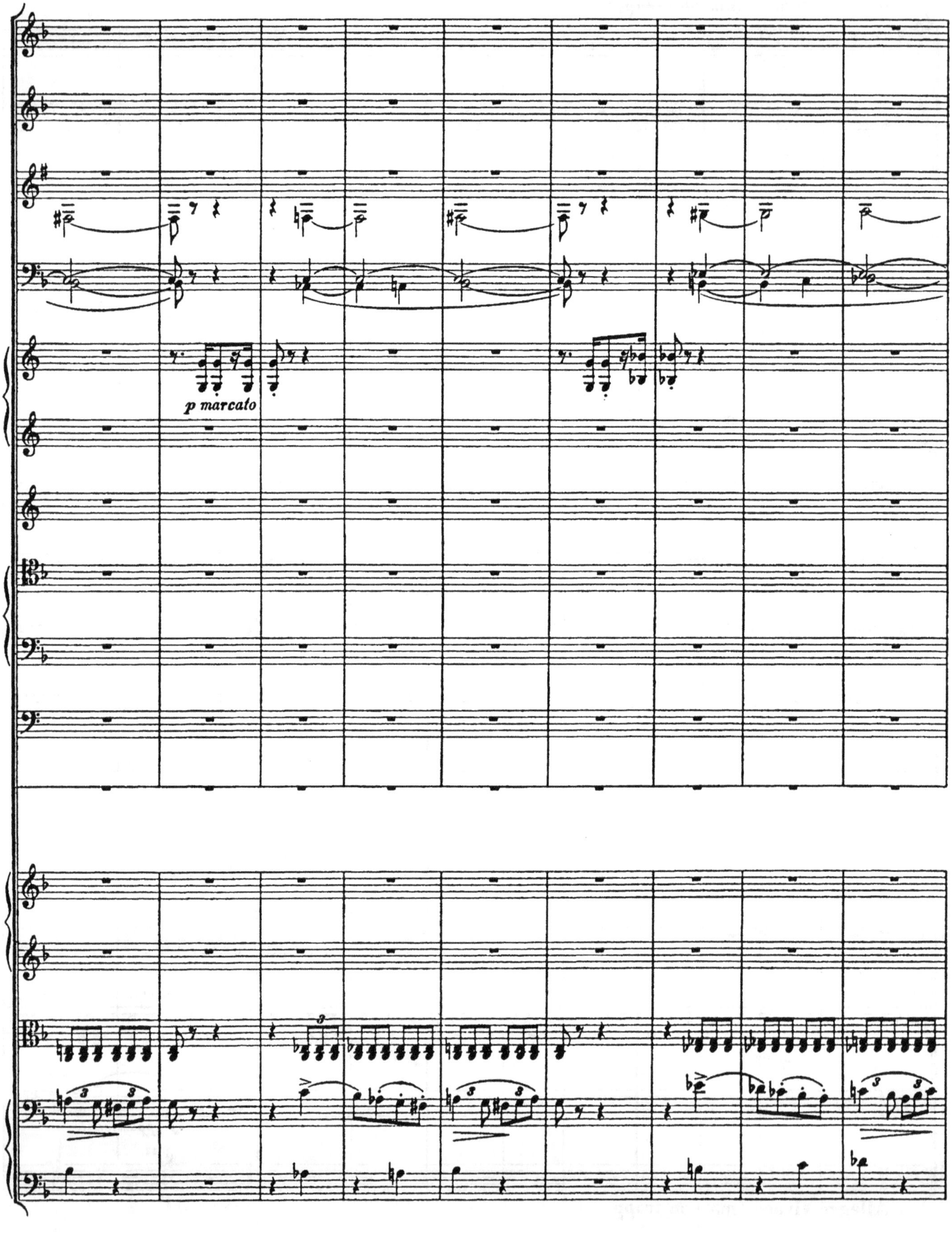
p marcato

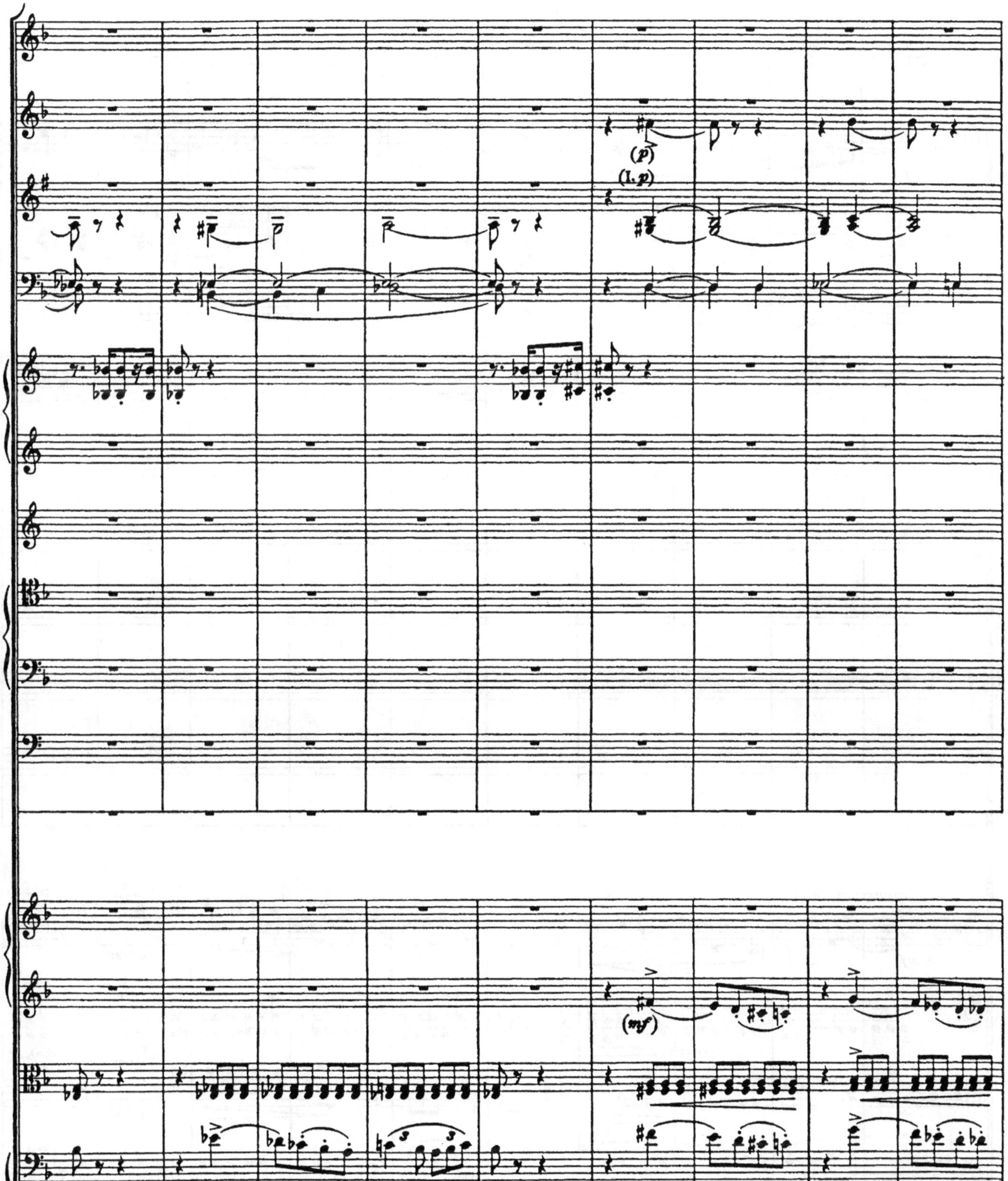
(p)
(1. p)
(mf)

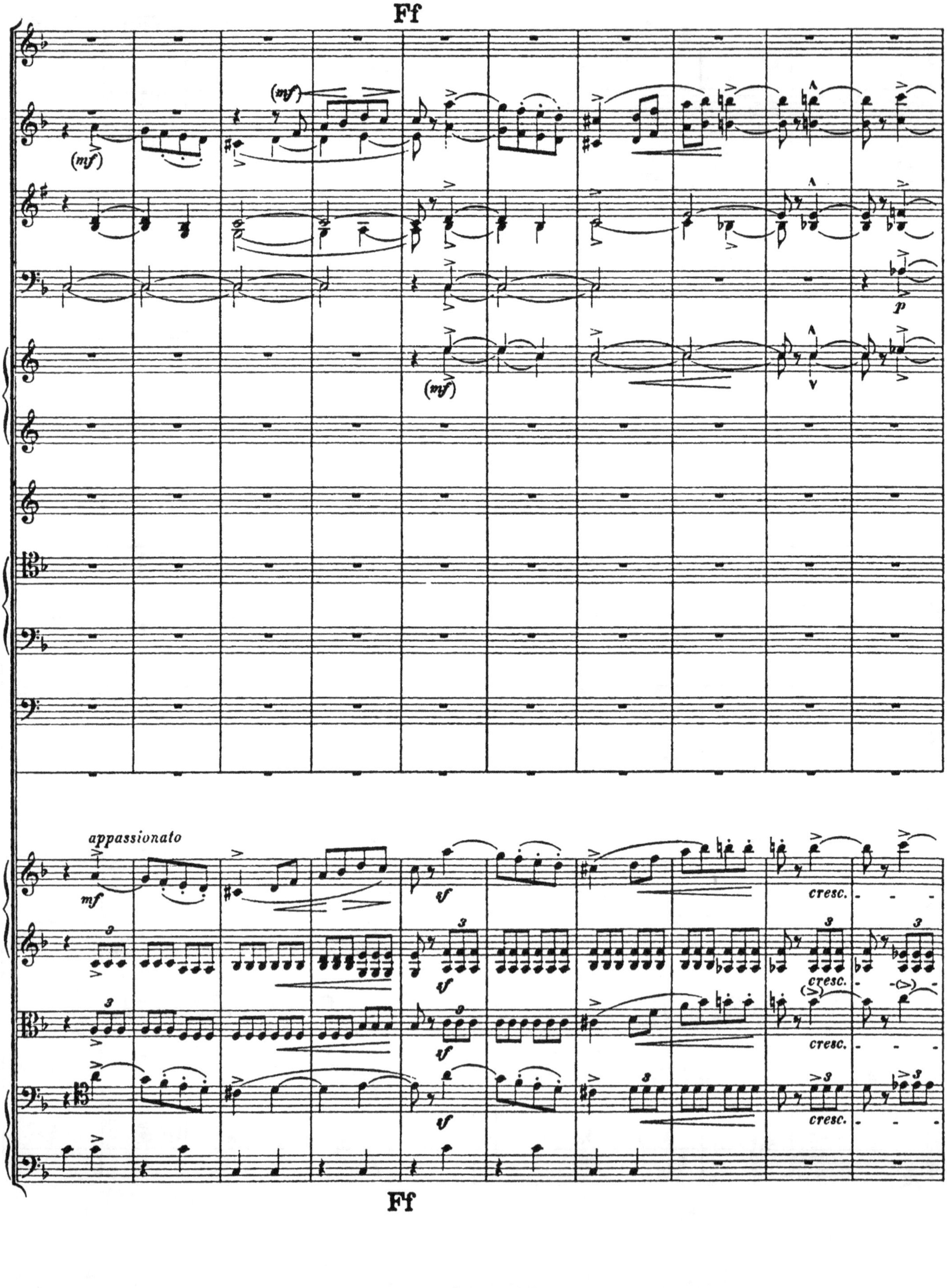
Ff
(mf)
(mf)
p
(mf)
appassionato
mf
sf
cresc.
Ff

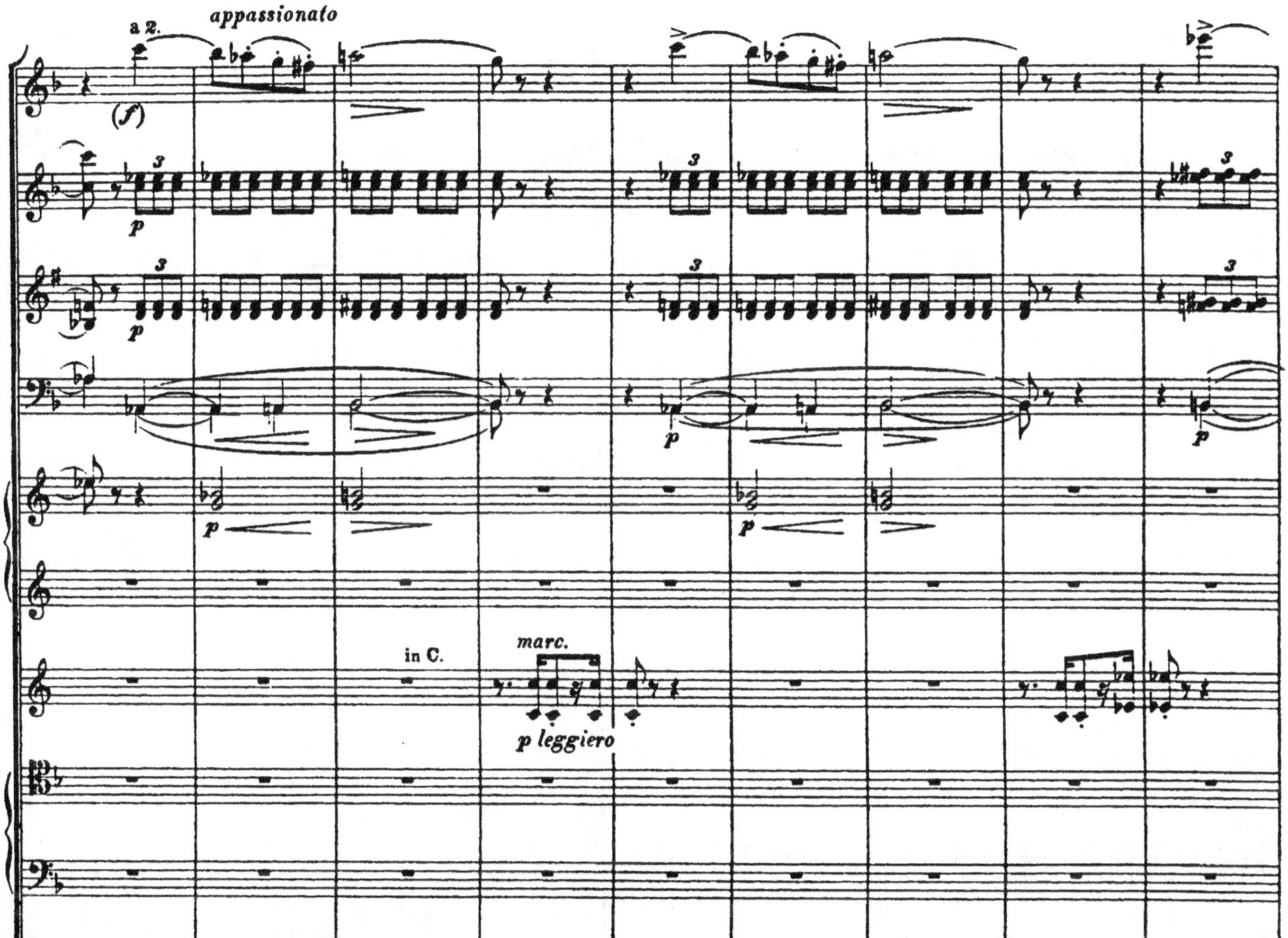
a 2.
appassionato
(f)
p
p
p
p
p
p
p
in C.
marc.
p leggiero
arco
(p)

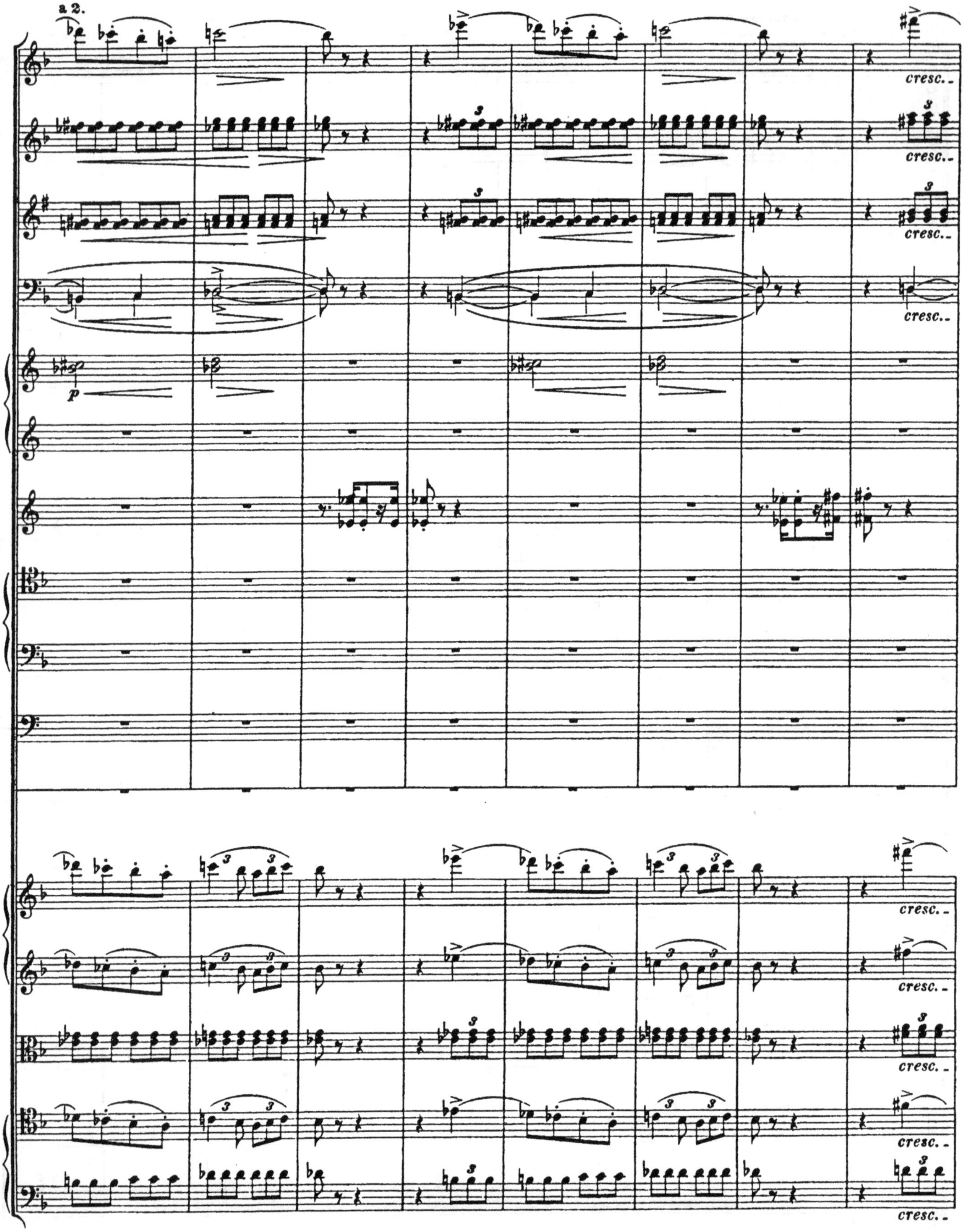
a 2.
cresc.
p

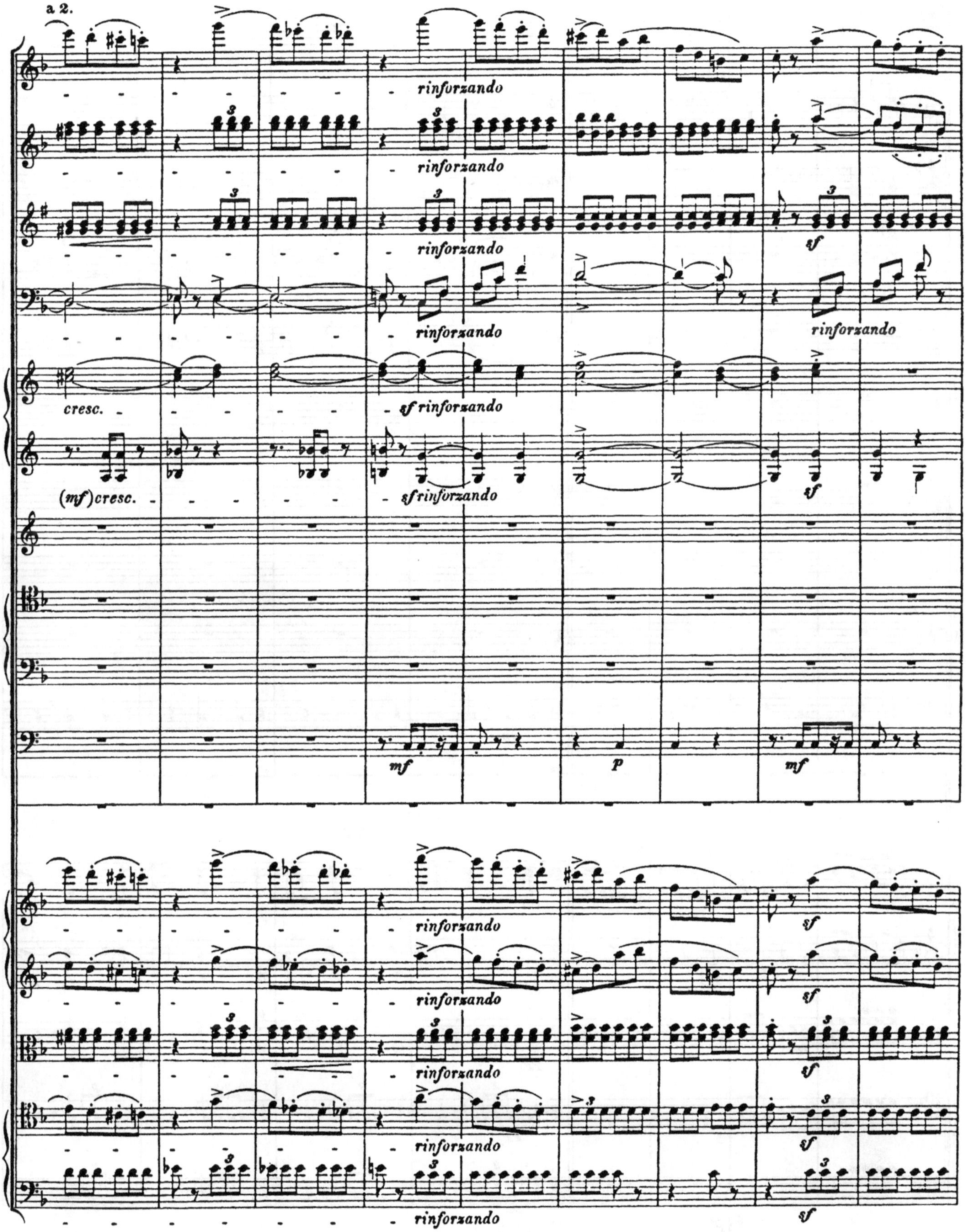
a 2.
rinforzando
cresc.
sf rinforzando
(mf) cresc.
sf
mf
p

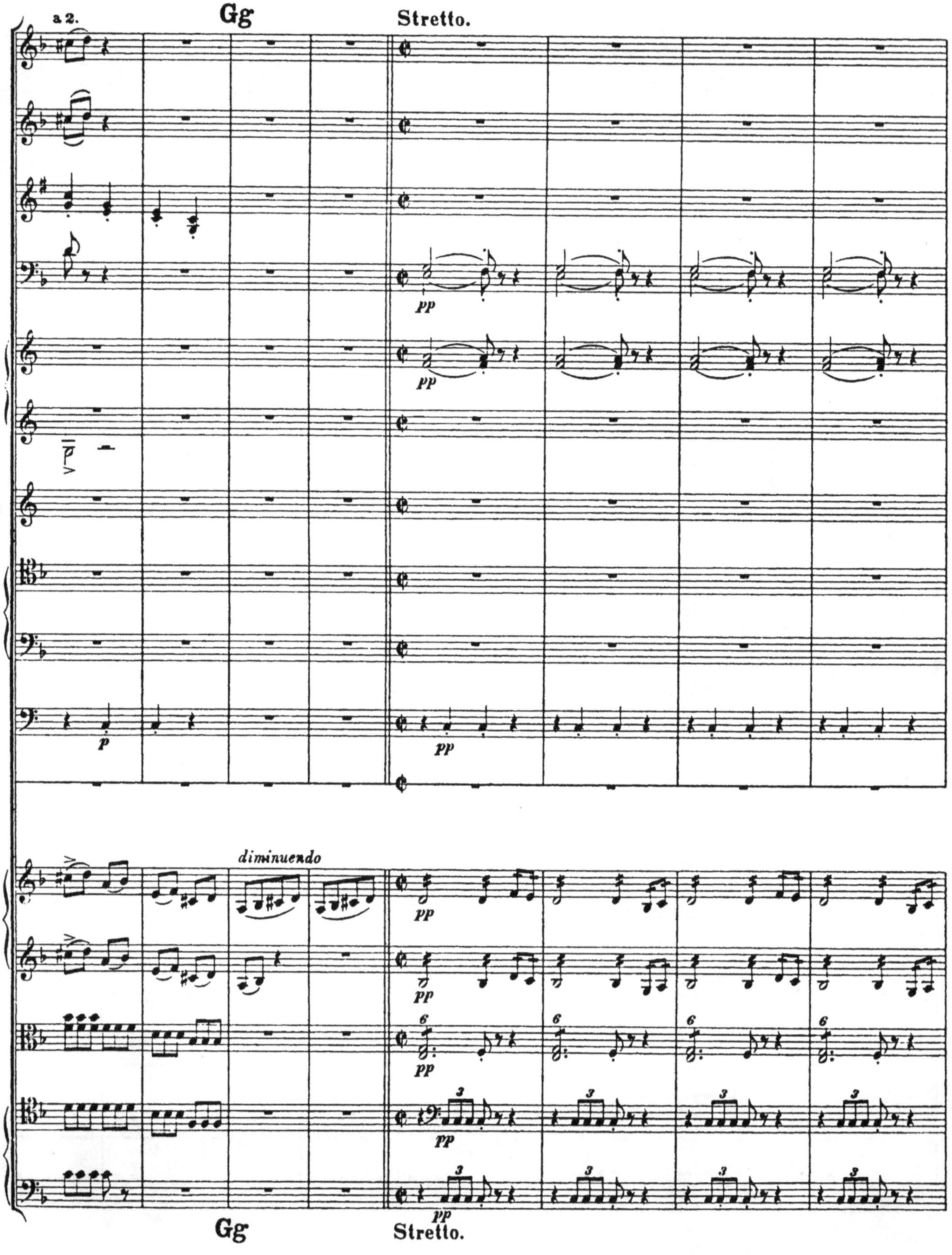
a 2.
Gg
Stretto.
p
pp
diminuendo
6
3
Gg
Stretto.

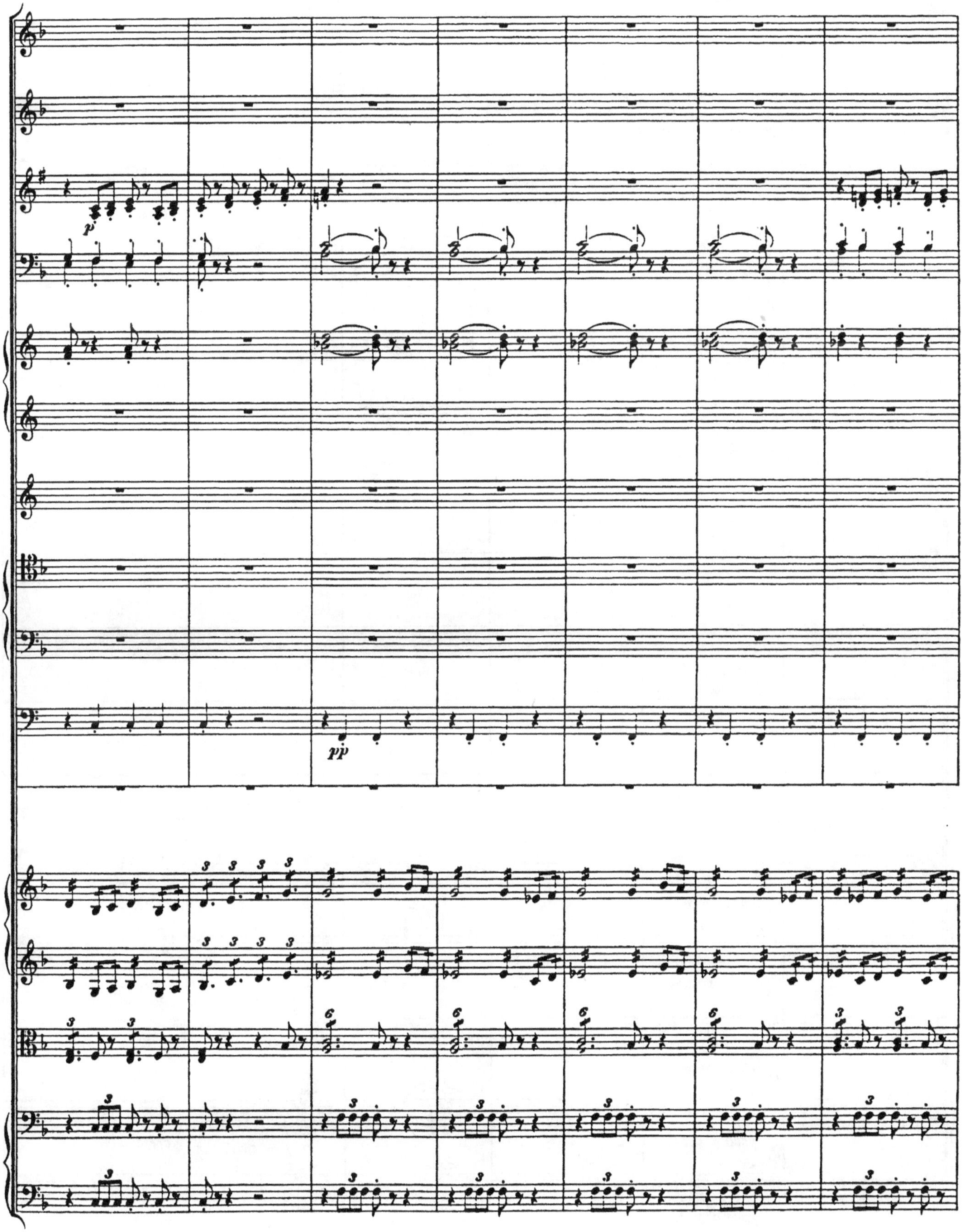
p
pp

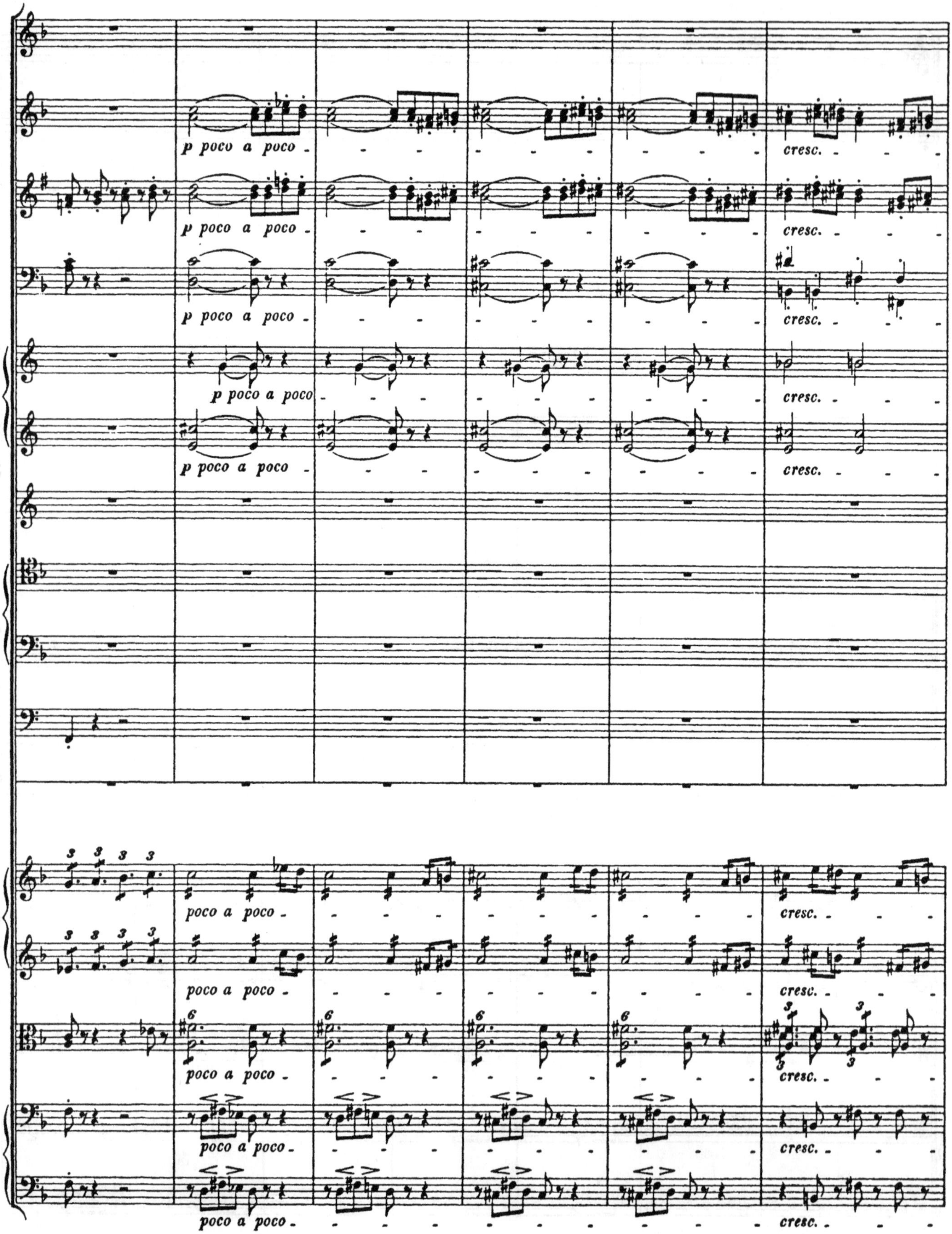
p poco a poco
cresc.
poco a poco
cresc.

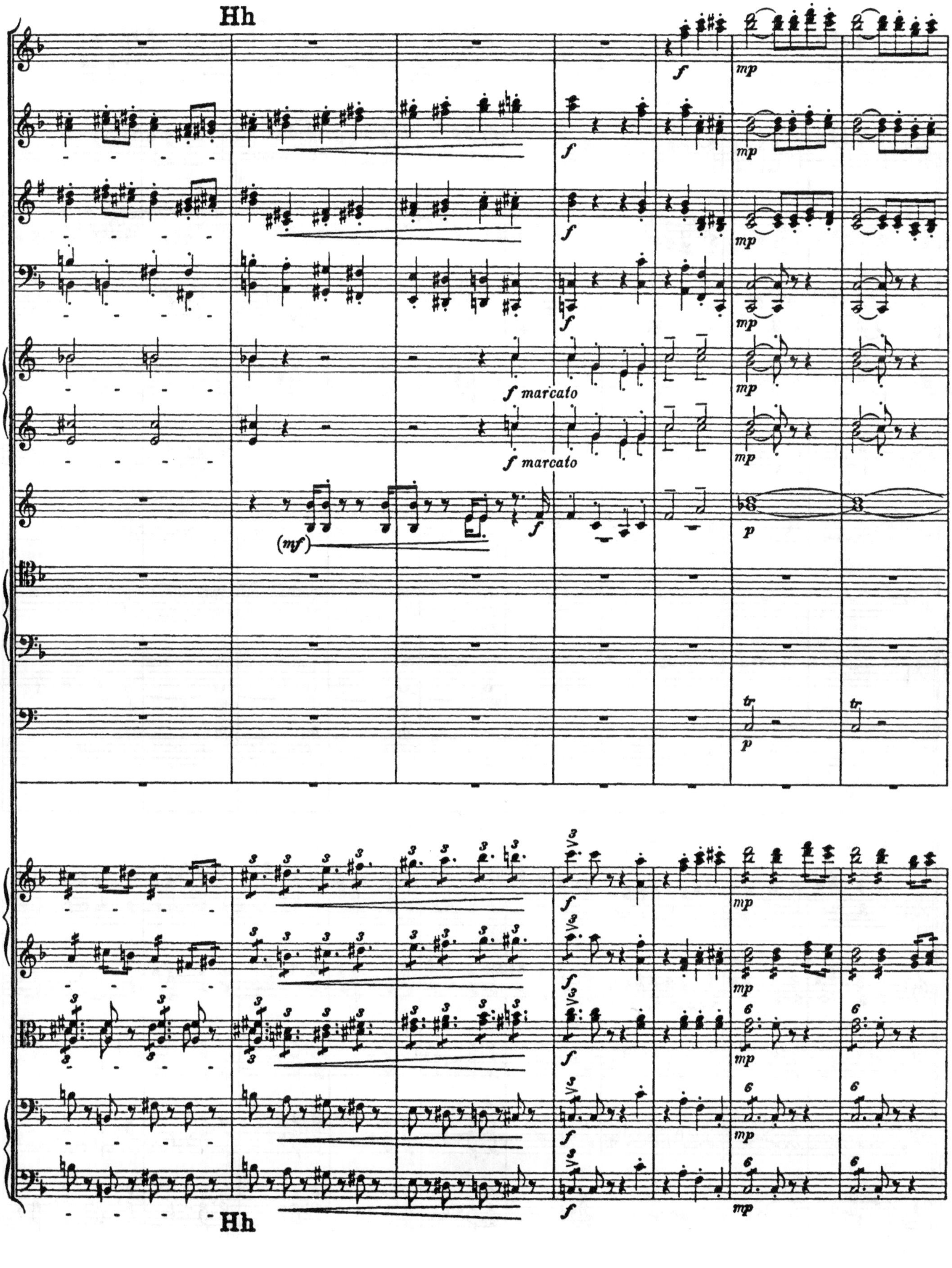
Hh
f marcato
f marcato
(mf)
tr
tr
Hh

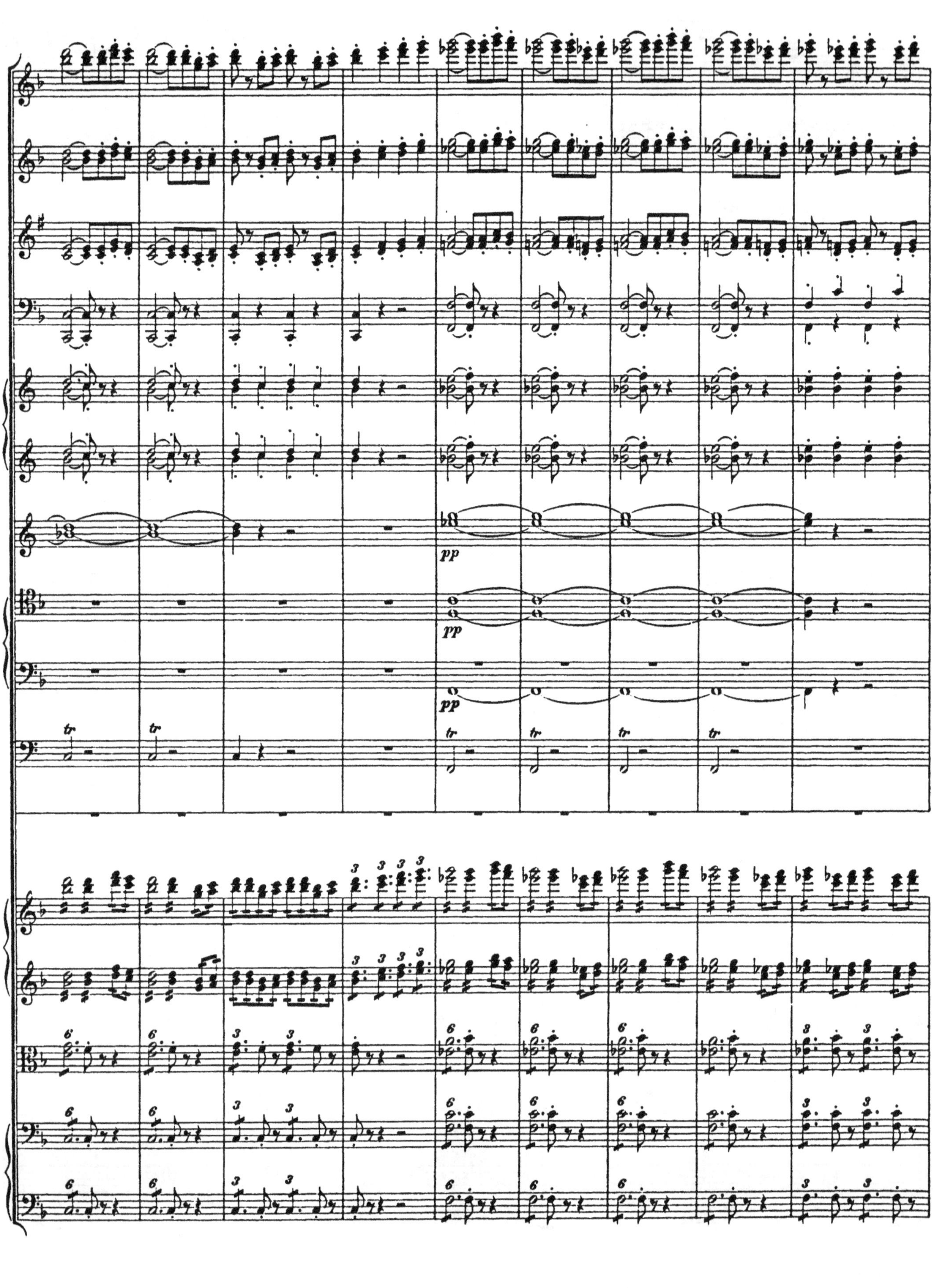
tr
pp

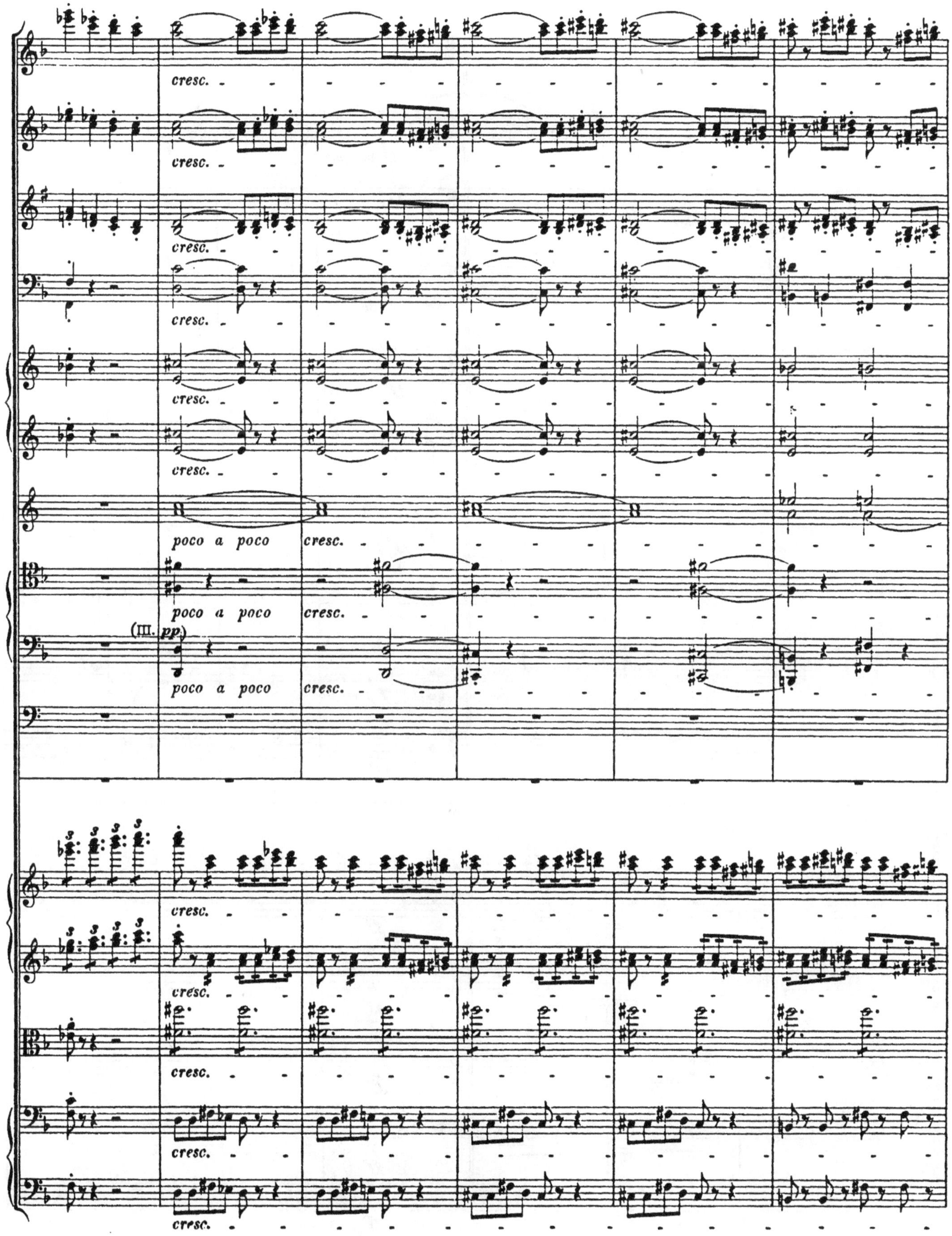
cresc.
poco a poco cresc.
(III. pp)

Ii
ff pomposo
ff pomposo
ff pomposo
ff pomposo
ff pomposo
ff pomposo
ff pomposo
ff pomposo
(f)
(ff)
ff
ff
ff
ff
ff
Ii

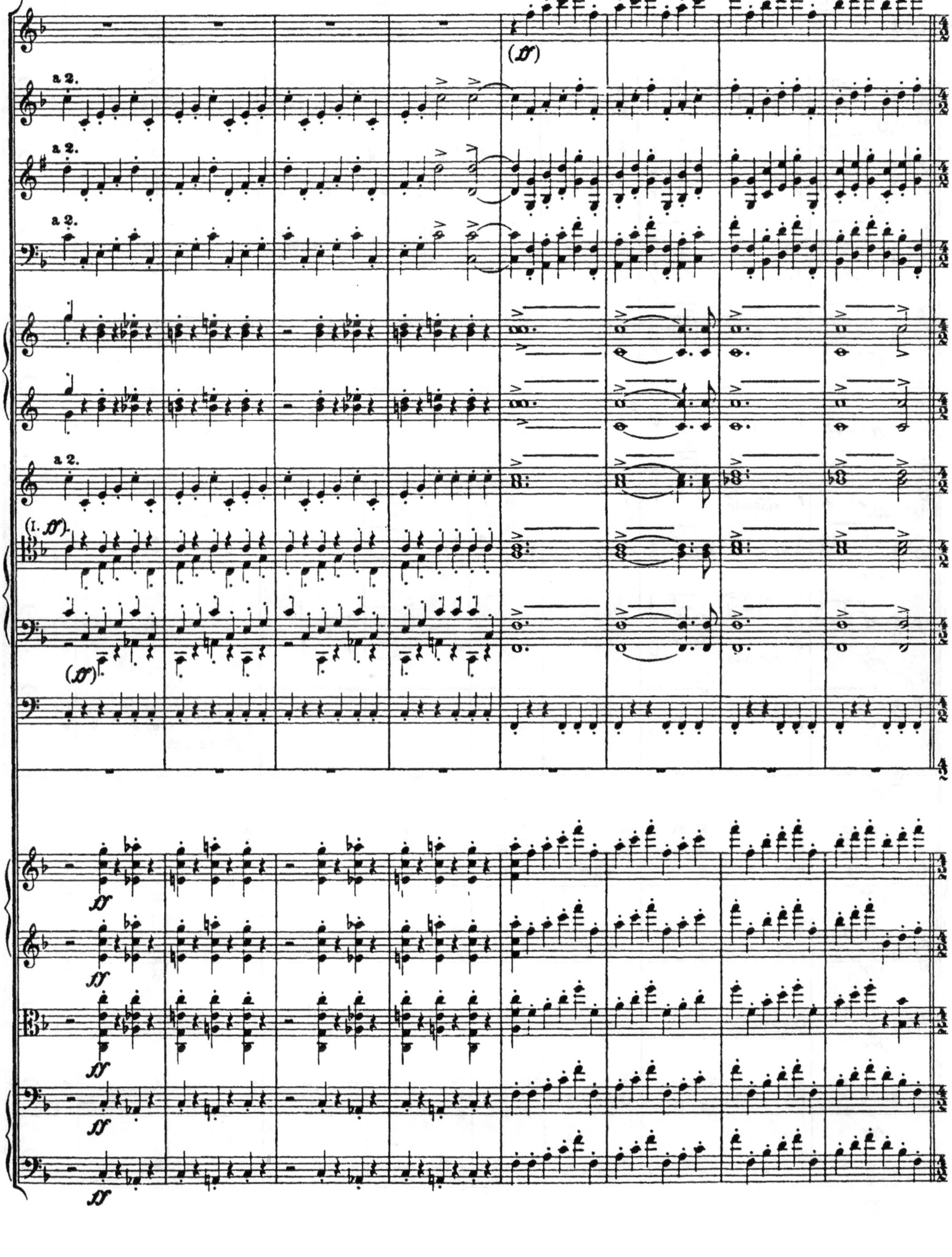
a 2.
(ff)
a 2.
a 2.
a 2.
a 2.
(I. ff)
(ff)
ff
ff
ff
ff
ff

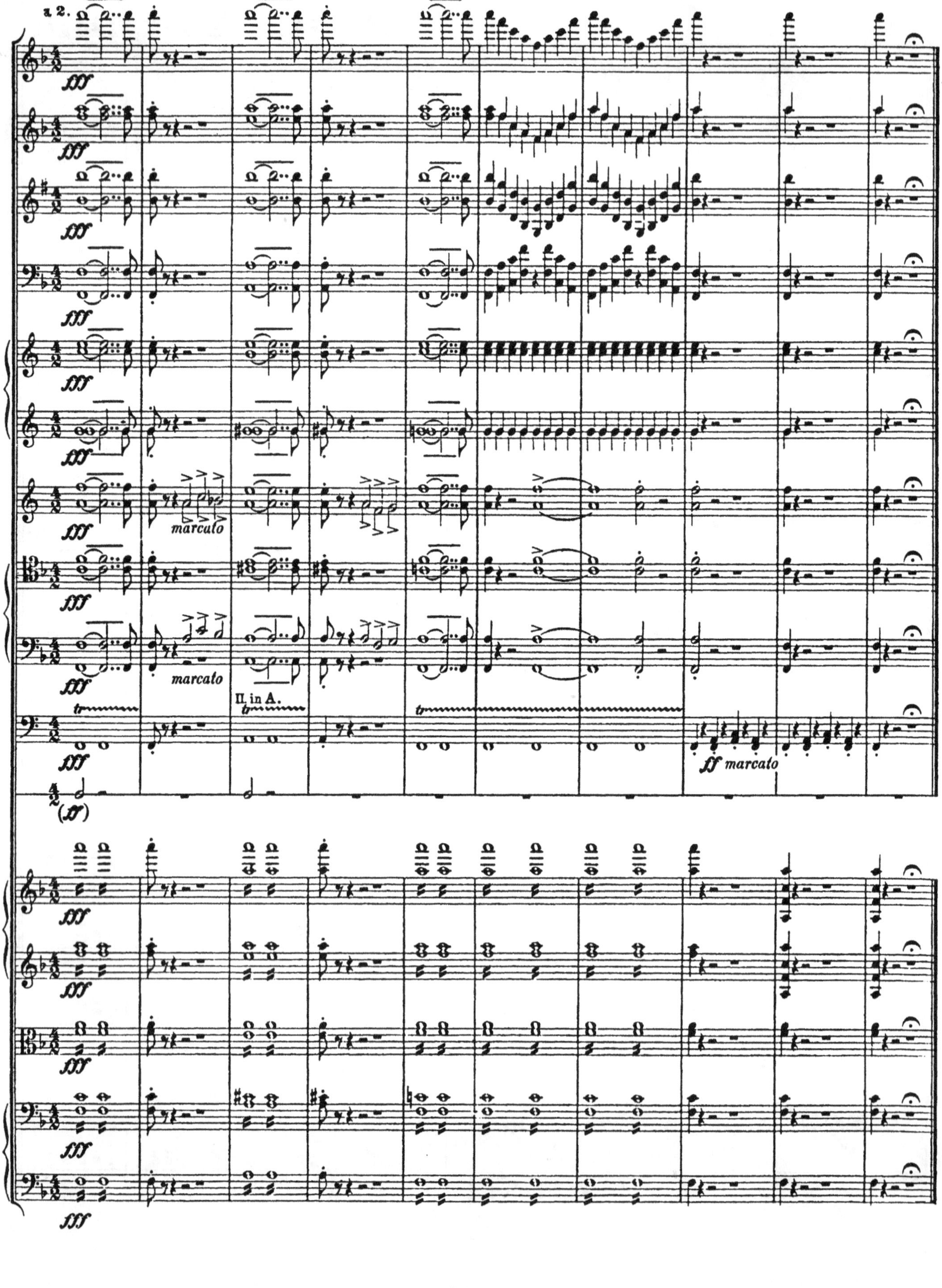
a 2.
fff
marcato
marcato
II. in A.
ff marcato
(ff)

Kürzung. Abbreviation. Abréviation.

Nötigenfalls kann folgende Kürzung stattfinden: Vom ersten Takte Seite 100, anstatt Seite 101, diese Ueberleitungstakte zum *Stretto* Seite 112, Takt 5.

If necessary, the following cut can be made: from the first bar of page 100 to the Stretto, page 112, bar 5, using these bars as a link.

En cas de besoin on pourrait abréger le passage en passant de la 1re mesure page 100 à page 112, mesure 5. *(Stretto).*

FRANZ LISZTS
SYMPHONISCHE DICHTUNGEN 11 u. 12

REVISIONSBERICHT

Im Jahre 1908 wurden in einer gemeinschaftlichen Sitzung der Revisoren, der Herausgeber und der Verleger die Leitgedanken und Grundsätze für eine vollständige, einheitliche und korrekte Gesamtausgabe der Werke Franz Liszts beraten und endgültig festgesetzt.

Aus praktischen Gründen der modernen Musikpflege mußten die vielfachen Unterschiede in der Benennung und Anordnung der Instrumente, in den Schlüsseln usw., vor allem aber sehr viele, für heutige Begriffe überflüssige oder selbst störende Versetzungszeichen beseitigt werden. Die auf letztere bezügliche Bestimmung lautet in endgültiger Fassung:

»Die von Liszt sehr reichlich angewendeten zufälligen Versetzungszeichen (namentlich Auflösungszeichen) sind für die heutige Praxis zum Teil entbehrlich geworden. Die nicht unbedingt notwendigen sind nur da beizubehalten, wo sie das Lesen tatsächlich noch erleichtern, Mißverständnisse verhüten oder für das harmonische Bild Lisztscher Schreibweise besonders charakteristisch erscheinen.«

Um jede Willkür auszuschliessen, sind alle irgendwie nennenswerten Änderungen, Weglassungen, Zusätze im Wortlaut der Lisztschen Partitur im Revisionsbericht je bei der betreffenden Komposition besonders aufgeführt und begründet worden, sodaß jeder mit der alten und der neuen Ausgabe in der Hand sich sein Urteil selbst bilden kann. Alle Zutaten, insbesondere Vortragsbezeichnungen, wurden in Klammern ( ) oder [ ] gesetzt; in einzelnen Fällen kann und soll dies nachträglich noch geschehen.

Die Herausgabe der Symphonischen Dichtungen war ursprünglich von Herrn Eugen d'Albert übernommen worden, der jedoch wegen anderweitiger großer Inanspruchnahme zurücktrat, nachdem er den Stich aller 12 Werke nur in erster Lesung hatte beaufsichtigen können. Die genaue Nachprüfung übernahm in dankenswerter Weise Herr Otto Taubmann in Berlin, in stetem Einvernehmen mit dem Kustos des Liszt-Museums, Herrn Hofrat Dr. Obrist, als dem Obmann der Revisionskommission.

BAND 6

HUNNENSCHLACHT.

Symphonische Dichtung Nr. 11.

Vorlage: Die erste Partiturausgabe, erschienen 1861 bei Breitkopf & Härtel in Leipzig. Verlagsnummer 10160.

Bemerkungen:

S. 18. Die Vorschrift der gedruckten Vorlage ›in 3 Viertel taktieren‹ wurde durch Weglassung des ›in‹ in ein korrektes Deutsch gebracht.

S. 18, 1. Takt — S. 19, 2. Takt. In der gedruckten Vorlage findet sich für die beiden ersten Hörner die ungebräuchliche Notierung

, die in die übliche geändert wurde.

S. 45, 1. Takt heißt es in den I. Violinen in der gedruckten Vorlage:

das Achtel c (dritte Note) ist, wie ein Vergleich mit Flöten und Hoboen, sowie mit der Parallelstelle auf S. 47, 2. Takt zeigt, ein Fehler; es muß ein Sechzehntel mit vorhergehender Sechzehntelpause sein.

S. 45, 3. Takt fehlt für 1. und 2. Horn in der gedruckten Vorlage die nach Analogie der Takte 2 und 4 auf S. 43 als nötig anzusehende Vorschrift ›gestopft‹.

S. 49. Während bei allen Streicherstellen, die ›mit breitem Strich‹ gespielt werden sollen, sonst jede Note die durchaus verständliche Bezeichnung > hat, stehen in der gedruckten Vorlage über der I. und II. Violine im 4. und halben 5. Takt plötzlich Punkte. Auch die erste Stichvorlage hat Punkte, die von Liszt selbst ergänzt wurden. Aber er hat sicher nicht an die (übrigens auch erst vom Kopisten hinzugefügten) vorhergegangenen > gedacht.

S. 55 hat die gedruckte Vorlage im 4. Takt für 3. und 4. Horn die augenscheinlich falsche Note (Klang b) statt des richtigen (Klang c); vergl. 2. Klar., 3. Tromp., 3. Posaune.

S. 61, 6. Takt wurde in der Orgel ein fehlender Bogen von as (¹/₂) zu as (¹/₄) in der Oberstimme ergänzt.

* * *

DIE IDEALE.

Symphonische Dichtung Nr. 12.

Vorlage: 1. Die erste Partiturausgabe, erschienen 1858 bei Breitkopf & Härtel. Verlagsnummer 9788.

2. Kürzungen, zusammen mit dem Anhang zu den Festklängen, 1861 erschienen. Verlagsnummer 10176.

Bemerkungen:

S. 21. Die Bezeichnung des Violoncell-Eintritts im 2. Takt mit der Angabe ›Solo‹ für die Oberstimme läßt es zweifelhaft erscheinen, ob nur ein Spieler die Oberstimme, oder ob die Hälfte aller Spieler sie ›mit solistischem Vortrage‹ wiedergeben soll. Vielleicht gibt die erste Stichvorlage einen Anhalt, in der sich von der Hand des Kopisten der Vermerk findet: { Solo / die übrigen Vcelle.

S. 30. Die Bögen über den Triolen der Streicher stehen zum größten Teil nicht in der gedruckten Vorlage. Ihre Hinzufügung trotz der Vorschrift ›legatissimo sempre‹ wurde indessen nicht für überflüssig erachtet.

S. 42. Die gedruckte Vorlage hat im 4. Takt unter den ersten Violoncellen ein ——< >——, das ersichtlich zu den zweiten Violoncellen gehört. Der Fehler stammt aus einer Undeutlichkeit der ersten Stichvorlage, in der das ——< >—— dicht über dem II. Violoncellen steht, was dann augenscheinlich falsch gedeutet wurde.

S. 46, 6. Takt steht in der gedruckten Vorlage für die I. Violine

. Das untere b ist als augenscheinlicher Stichfehler (siehe vorher und nachher) gestrichen worden.

S. 65, 2. Takt gilt für den Violoncell-Einsatz das über den gleichen Fall auf S. 21 Gesagte.

S. 72. Die sprachlich mangelhafte Vorschrift der gedruckten Vorlage ›im ³/₄ taktieren‹ wurde geändert in ›drei Schläge im Takt‹.

S. 79. Die sprachlich mangelhafte Vorschrift der gedruckten Vorlage ›im ²/₄ taktieren‹ wurde geändert in ›zwei Schläge im Takt‹.

S. 97. In der gedruckten Vorlage lautet der fünfte Takt in den Trompeten so:

Der Bogen von der Halben f zum c in der I. Trompete ist als Stichfehler entfernt worden; er steht auch nicht in der ersten Stichvorlage.

Eugen d'Albert   Otto Taubmann
Berlin.   Berlin.

Dr. Aloys Obrist
Weimar.

www.ingramcontent.com/pod-product-compliance
Lightning Source LLC
Chambersburg PA
CBHW081233090426
42738CB00016B/3288